HAVE

YOU EVER

WONDERED?

Edited by

ANDY BANNISTER
GAVIN MATTHEWS

HAVE

Finding the *Everyday Clues to*

YOU EVER

Meaning,

WONDERED?

Purpose & Spirituality

a division of 10ofthose.com

British Library Cataloguing in Publication Data
A record for this book is available from the British Library

ISBN: 9781915705488

Designed by Jude May
Cover image © MicroStockHub | iStock

Printed in Denmark

10Publishing, a division of 10ofthose.com
Unit C, Tomlinson Road, Leyland, PR25 2DY, England
Email: info@10ofthose.com
Website: www.10ofthose.com

3 5 7 10 8 6 4 2

In memory of Jeff Howarth

Contents

Introduction   Why wonder?
Gavin Matthews   1

1   Have you ever wondered why we long for happiness?
    Andy Bannister   5

2   Have you ever wondered why the best stories are about
    good and evil?
    Andy Bannister   9

3   Have you ever wondered why we love happy endings?
    Gavin Matthews   13

4   Have you ever wondered why humans are attracted to
    the supernatural?
    Gareth Black   17

5   Have you ever wondered why we crave money despite
    knowing it's not the answer?
    Andy Moore   21

6   Have you ever wondered why we are drawn to beauty?
    Mary Jo Sharp   25

7   Have you ever wondered why we hate selfishness and
    admire altruism?
    Andy Bannister   29

8 Have you ever wondered why the environment matters?
   Andy Steiger   35

9 Have you ever wondered why mathematics works?
   Andy Bannister   39

10 Have you ever wondered why music has the power to move us?
    Michael Ots   45

11 Have you ever wondered why humans are so incurably curious?   51
    Mary Jo Sharp

12 Have you ever wondered why black lives matter?   55
    Clare Williams

13 Have you ever wondered why we find loneliness so difficult?
    Michael Ots   59

14 Have you ever wondered why we treat sex as something sacred?   63
    Anne Witton

15 Have you ever wondered what love is?
    Gareth Black   67

16 Have you ever wondered if your life is worthwhile?
    Clare Williams   71

17 Have you ever wondered why we preserve the past?
    Anne Witton   75

18 Have you ever wondered who you really are?
    Michael Ots   81

Contents

19 Have you ever wondered why suffering and evil seem so wrong?
David Nixon   85

20 Have you ever wondered why we long for justice?
Clare Williams   89

21 Have you ever wondered what happens when you die?
Anne Witton   93

22 Have you ever wondered if you're a good or a bad person?
Andy Bannister   97

23 Have you ever wondered if you were created for a purpose?
David Nixon   103

24 Have you ever wondered what God thinks of you?
David Nixon   109

25 Have you ever wondered if Jesus actually existed?
David Nixon   115

26 Have you ever wondered if all religions are basically the same?
Andy Bannister   121

27 Have you ever wondered where everything is going?
Gavin Matthews   127

28 Have you ever wondered if you can truly change?
Gareth Black   133

Conclusion   Have you ever wondered where to look for answers?
Andy Bannister   139

Endnotes   145

Contributors   155

Acknowledgements   159

Introduction

Why wonder?

Gavin Matthews

'He who can no longer pause to wonder and stand rapt in awe, is as good as dead; his eyes are closed.' Albert Einstein

It was Marilyn Monroe who declared: 'We human beings are strange creatures.' She had a point. Alone among the animals inhabiting the earth, the task of asking 'Why?' has fallen to us. Blackbirds are content to sing, cows to chew the cud, and rabbits to, well, breed like rabbits. Even the higher mammals such as monkeys and dolphins seem completely unburdened by questions of meaning.

But we humans simply can't stop wondering about our experiences. Even as we do ordinary things like eat, sleep, work, pay taxes, and raise children, 'Why?' questions haunt our steps. And as Plato remarked:

This feeling of wonder shows that you are a philosopher, since wonder is the only beginning of philosophy.

That's why I consider the aforementioned Marilyn Monroe to be a philosopher, and so are you—because you are *wired to wonder*.

This is a book all about wondering. But it's not a dusty academic book, nor is it loaded with technical lingo or arcane arguments. Rather it's about the thoughts and questions we all experience when we encounter the mystery and complexity of this world.

Have you ever looked at a sunset and pondered why it is so profoundly moving? Or perhaps considered why we long for justice and rail against suffering and evil, but respect and honour self-sacrifice? It's profoundly odd behaviour, to say the least, if we're little more than competing gene-machines seeking to be the fittest and survive.

Love is a funny thing too, isn't it? Clearly, it's linked with the need to reproduce but there's so much more to it than simply passing on our DNA. Even sex itself tends to get treated as something sacred, rather than purely a biological function. Have you ever wondered why? If you have, then this is the book for you.

We begin with some of the most broad and foundational wonderings that we all experience, and then zero in on some more specific questions towards the end, providing a progression from one chapter to the next. Each chapter also works as a stand-alone piece and makes sense on its own, allowing you to dive right into the topics which grab you most.

When I commissioned this project, I invited a range of contributors to collaborate and to write about the questions which have most captured their imaginations. I was delighted by the responses I received—and am hugely grateful to all those who are featured here in this book. These men and women come from a wide range of backgrounds: science, law, linguistics, communication, theology, comparative religion, bioethics, history, and more. What they all have in common is that their wonderings have led them to a profoundly Christian spirituality. This doesn't mean what they explore will only be of interest to people who come to the same conclusions though. This book is for anyone who has looked at a landscape and contemplated why we are so drawn to beauty, or questioned why we humans are so insatiably curious about our universe, or even for those who have simply looked up at a million stars in a vast black night's sky and just *wondered*.

Have You Ever Wondered? invites you to sit back and enjoy being human, to appreciate once again the multi-sensory extravaganza of the cosmos, from the order that makes mathematics work, to the fascinating sense of self-awareness we experience. This book also urges you onwards, to embrace these wonderings and to see where these questions might lead. After all, pondering why the world *is* as it *is*, leads us onto wondering if it is as it *ought* to be, and then if *we* are as we ought to be. And if not, what might be done? It explores how so much of what we think and feel points to deeper spiritual realities.

It is wonder-full to be human, with this unique capacity to question, to ask, and to imagine. So, along with my sincere thanks to all who have contributed to this volume, and to 10Publishing, may I invite you to open these pages and wonder awhile.

1

Have you ever wondered why we long for happiness?

Andy Bannister

We inhabit a happiness obsessed culture. Every day, a million Westerners type 'happiness' into Google. There are thousands of books telling you how to find happiness, multiple podcasts discussing it, and any number of movies and songs all about it. Coming of age in the 90s, I can still remember the cheerful bubble-gum flavoured lyrics of R.E.M.'s classic 'Shiny Happy People'.

But why do we humans pursue happiness? After all, the rest of the animal kingdom seems pretty content with just the biological basics: survival and reproduction. But humans? We need so much more than merely the bare necessities of life. What is going on here?

As we ponder this question, perhaps the first thing to explore is what exactly we mean by the word 'happiness'. Ask most people, 'Do you want to be happy?' and of course they'll say

'Yes!' But inquire, 'What do you mean by happy?' and that's a bit tougher to answer. The ancient Greek philosopher Aristotle once suggested that there are actually four levels of happiness and to be truly happy, we need to ensure that we are living at all four levels.[1]

Happiness level 1 is basically animal happiness and involves fulfilling your appetites. So, for example, I see the chocolate doughnut. I eat the doughnut. I am happy. I feel good—and I can, of course, if it's a box of six and my wife isn't watching, repeat this exercise. Eventually though, the happiness will be over (and probably over with a side helping of nausea).

The same is true of that other appetite, sex. In the context of committed love, sex can be amazing. But abuse it, for example treating the other person as a means rather than an end, then a great deal of unhappiness can result. Indeed, if you misuse any of your appetites—eating to cope with anxiety, or having transient one-night stands to cope with loneliness or boredom—you will soon end up deeply unhappy. And if you're unhappy at level 1, suggested Aristotle, the only way is up, to level 2.

Happiness level 2 is all about comparison, about having more or being better than the next person. There's nothing inherently wrong with developing a skill and using it well. Excelling in sport, succeeding at work, coming top of the class: all that can bring happiness. But be warned: you won't be at the top for ever. Indeed, trying to live entirely at happiness level 2 can be deeply stressful, as you worry what happens when you're no longer the fastest, smartest, or whatever. And even when you do win, sometimes the victory can seem hollow. In the movie *Cool Runnings*, about the Jamaican bobsleigh team's debut at the 1988 Winter Olympics, the coach (played by John Candy) wisely says to the team: 'A gold medal is a wonderful thing. But if you're not enough without it, you'll never be enough with it.'

When happiness level 2 lets you down, you need to move up to level 3. Happiness level 3, said Aristotle, is all about living for somebody other than yourself. One prime example would be parenting; pouring your time and energy into caring for children. Alternatively, you can serve others by donating your time, money, or talents to help those around you. But the problem is that these things also come to an end. Those you care for will one day no longer need you. And if you're not careful, this approach to life can subtly become profoundly selfish—possibly without even realising it, your motivations can morph from wanting to help others to wanting to feel good or look good in front of others.

So where now? If happiness levels 1 through 3 don't ultimately satisfy us, presumably the only way is up? At the top of this ladder lies our last hope, happiness level 4. To paraphrase our old friend Aristotle, level 4 comes when you connect to an ultimate source of happiness outside of yourself.

This reminds me of something that Jesus of Nazareth once taught. Jesus had much to say about happiness, often highlighting our tendency to look for it in all the wrong places. Seeing how our search has disappointed and drained us, Jesus said: 'Come to me, all you who are weary and burdened, and I will give you rest.'[2]

The basic problem with happiness levels 1 through 3 is that *we* bear the weight of the effort— we exhaust ourselves trying to reach that ever elusive goal of happiness, only to watch it constantly recede into the distance, like the end of a rainbow. Trying to find happiness this way will drive you to craziness or cynicism or, more likely, both.

But Jesus offers us something refreshingly different. For Jesus claimed to be God himself, stepping into space and time and history. As the very one who made us, he is also the one who knows what we really need, what we were truly designed for.

There is nothing inherently wrong with food and sex, sport and success, generosity and self-giving. But they can never ultimately satisfy us. And for a very good reason: we were made for so much more. Jesus said, 'I have come that [people] may have life, and have it to the full'.[3] When we encounter him, we discover something infinitely more than a happiness whose shine quickly fades; we discover a joy that nothing and no one can ever take away from us.

2

Have you ever wondered why the best stories are about good and evil?

Andy Bannister

A strong contender for the most well-known phrase in the English language must be: 'Once upon a time ...' Whether we are children or adults, we *love* stories; indeed our love of stories is something uniquely human. From the earliest recorded cave paintings to the latest movie, across time, country, and culture, humans are a storytelling species.

Some stories are here today and gone tomorrow but others become classics, retold for generations. When a story is first written, it's hard to tell whether it will become a classic but I would suggest that one thing most of the greatest stories have in common is they are built around a common theme: the triumph of good over evil.[1]

Whether it's Katniss bringing down the establishment in *The Hunger Games*, the defeat of Sauron in *The Lord of the Rings*, or the fight against the Empire in *Star Wars*, or Harry Potter versus Voldemort, good over evil stories abound. The list of examples could go on almost endlessly. For sure there's some dystopian fiction out there; but in almost all the classic stories, evil always gets a good kicking. In our most loved, most enduring stories, good wins.

But have you ever wondered *why*? After all, if we live in a godless universe, all that matters is survival and reproduction. The only truthful story in this case would be something like *The Little DNA Molecule That Could*, which I suspect would be somewhat lacking in the plot department.

Not merely do we love stories, despite their total uselessness to the whole he-who-passes-on-his-DNA-the-most-successfully-wins game, but in a godless universe, they're not only useless, they're a load of old rubbish, aren't they? First, because 'good' and 'evil' are meaningless categories in a world which just consists of atoms in motion. Morality is just a nice story for children—but grown-ups need to have the courage to say 'Bah, humbug!' to all that. On top of which, in a godless universe, the grim truth is that good doesn't triumph. It simply *doesn't*. Chaos wins in the end: suffering and death await all of us and the story of *your* life is the same as everybody else's: 'Born. Suffered. Died.' So in a godless universe, our love of stories where good wins is merely delusion, wish-fulfilment, or brilliant marketing by publishers.

My guess is that this conclusion doesn't sit well with many of us. Could it be that we're drawn to these classic stories because deep in our very bones we know that they resonate with reality? That in some way we sense they are reflections of the one true story?

The theme of good triumphing over evil is, of course, profoundly Christian. It is the theme that runs through the whole of the Bible culminating in the story of Jesus and his victory over the forces of darkness. That Christian storyline is reflected in many of our favourite stories, sometimes deliberately, sometimes accidently. For example, Tolkien wrote:

> The Lord of the Rings *is of course a fundamentally religious and Catholic work; unconsciously so at first, but consciously in the revision.*[2]

While in a 2007 interview, J. K. Rowling explained how the *Harry Potter* books were deeply influenced by her faith.[3] Then the *Star Wars* stories contain many Christian ideas: just think of the sacrifice of Obi-Wan Kenobi in *A New Hope*, for example.

If Christianity is the true story of how a good God created a good world for human beings; of how we were corrupted by greed and power; and of how God stepped into creation to rescue us at the cost of his own life, it should not surprise us that human beings engage in our God-given role of 'sub-creation'.[4] When we create stories of our own, we naturally find that these reflect the One True Story.

But one last thought. It's been suggested that you can divide most of the world's stories into two types: comedies and tragedies. A tragedy is a story which begins with all going well and then ends in *catastrophe* for somebody. (Think Shakespeare's *Macbeth* and the titular character's downward spiral into murder and insanity.) If you graphed the trajectory of a tragedy, it would look like a frown. By contrast, the graph of a comedy looks like a smile—it seems all has gone wrong, but then comes a dramatic turn of events and the story climbs up to victory (or what Tolkien called *eucatastrophe*).

If atheism is true, if we live in a godless universe, then we are living in a tragedy. No matter how high humanity may squirm up the greasy pole of existence, everything ends in ruin. But if Christianity is true, then no matter how dark things may look, we know that this is not the story's end. Evil will be ultimately defeated and, long after the last tear has fallen, only that which is good remains. As Sam Gamgee said to Frodo in the film adaptation of *The Two Towers*:

> *It's like in the great stories Mr. Frodo. The ones that really mattered. Full of darkness and danger they were, and sometimes you didn't want to know the end. Because how could the end be happy? How could the world go back to the way it was when so much bad happened? But in the end, it's only a passing thing, this shadow. Even darkness must pass. A new day will come. And when the sun shines it will shine out the clearer. Those were the stories that stayed with you. That meant something. Even if you were too small to understand why.*

I believe that our love of stories was wired deeply into us by the God who created us, as one more clue, one more pointer to who we really are and for what—indeed for *whom*—we were really made. And so the question becomes, will we follow Ariadne's thread, the trail of the stones in the wood, the light from the lamppost—will we follow these clues where they lead? Or will we switch off the TV, close the book, and mutter 'it's all meaningless' to ourselves? Now that really *would* be a tragedy.

3

Have you ever wondered why we love happy endings?

Gavin Matthews

In 1996, Walt Disney created an animated musical of Victor Hugo's celebrated novel *The Hunchback of Notre Dame*. With starring voice-over roles given to A-listers like Demi Moore and Kevin Kline, and the iconic character of 'hunchback' Quasimodo to lead the narrative, it was an obvious blockbuster, and unsurprisingly grossed $325m at the box office. Disney clearly got something right!

Whether Victor Hugo would have approved of the *Disneyfication* of his story is more doubtful. Hugo ends his tale of rivalry, love and betrayal in shocking fashion. The evil Frollo frames the beautiful Esmerelda for his own crime, and laughs as she is executed. This provokes Quasimodo to kill him, by hurling him from the top of Notre Dame Cathedral. Quasimodo then starves himself to death in grief. Dark stuff indeed. Far too dark for Hollywood, at least.[1] In the Disney version Quasimodo rescues Esmerelda, and kills Frollo by accident, and is finally received into Parisienne society with jubilation—and singing!

To be fair to Disney, we *love* a happy ending—Elizabeth Bennet marries Mr Darcy, Inigo Montoya defeats the six-fingered man, Matilda gets to live with Miss Honey. Richard Curtis didn't just bring William Thacker and Anna Scott together at the end of *Notting Hill*, but ended his romcom with them dreamily awaiting the birth of their child. Happy endings are extraordinarily popular.

But why? After all, life in the real world is not like that most of the time. That is why relentless happy endings can sometimes feel saccharine or just *cheesy*, if you've experienced the brute realities of divorce, cancer, infertility or betrayal.

But even when life is hard for many, happy endings continue to sell. I suspect that the reason is more than escapism; these stories appeal to something deep within us, about the way we know the world *ought* to be. After all, the greatest happy endings do not come at the end of stories in which there has been unbridled joy throughout; but rather in those where obstacles, difficulties and disappointments have been overcome. The greater the tension, the greater the relief when resolution is found. If Johnny had easily beaten the bully, *The Karate Kid* would have fallen flat. It's the same with the perennial 'Will they / won't they?' of romance. Whether it's the years Audrey Tatou's character spends searching for her missing fiancé in *A Very Long Engagement*, or Audrey Hepburn's princess in *Roman Holiday*—separated from her co-star Gregory Peck by class and duty—we understand the longing and seeking for resolution found in these narratives, because they reflect reality. These stories bridge between the way the world is, and the hope we have for a world as it ought to be; played out in mini-dramas through characters we can relate to.

But are these happy endings realistic, or are they a joyful delusion? Which ending of *The Hunchback of Notre Dame* is the better story? Some people have said that any kind of optimism about life is treacherous ground. In his famous essay 'A Free Man's Worship', atheist philosopher Bertrand Russell writes:

> *Man['s] ... origin, his growth, his hopes and fears, his loves and his beliefs, are but the outcome of accidental collocations of atoms; that no fire, no heroism, no intensity of thought and feeling, can preserve an individual life beyond the grave; that all the labours of the ages, all the devotion, all the inspiration, all the noonday brightness of human genius, are destined to extinction in the vast death of the solar system, and that the whole temple of Man's achievement must inevitably be buried beneath the debris of a universe in ruins ... Only within the scaffolding of these truths, only on the firm foundation of unyielding despair, can the soul's habitation henceforth be safely built.[2]*

If Russell is correct then the universe is empty, there is no hope, all endings are tragedies, and any story which tells you otherwise is a lie. (This is presumably why Bertrand didn't pen any romcoms!) Yet it seems strange that, if despair is the grounding truth of reality, our whole culture and way we view the world is completely discordant with it.

Rather than resigning ourselves to a universe characterised by nothing more than 'blind pitiless indifference',[3] we long for resolutions in stories because we are all longing for the resolution to the mystery of our own lives. We are all hungry for redemption. Marty McFly simply *must* save his family from extinction and escape *Back to the Future*; he cannot simply accept being erased! James Bond surely *can't* die in his nemesis' lair, he *has* to bring the enemy down; Marianne Dashwood *can't* be left heartbroken; Aslan *can't* be defeated. We instinctively hope for some almost miraculous intervention, some external force to come in and set things straight. Bond needs a wondrous gadget to escape, Marianne needs a Colonel Brandon, and Aslan needs to rise from the dead. And this pattern of loss, hope and ultimate redemption seems to be woven into the very fabric of our view of the world.

Could this be because Western culture is thoroughly soaked in the Christian story: our law and education systems ooze biblical assumptions, while our media constantly uses biblical categories without realising that it is so doing?[4] Thus we respond to happy endings because we've been unconsciously shaped by the Christian story. When we hear a redemptive narrative—when all that seems lost is rescued—it chimes within us because it re-tells us a story we already instinctively and deeply believe.

The Bible's central story is of a hero who came to rescue a fallen world, but who was crucified by those he came to love. Yet while all his friends and family gave in to despair, Jesus's death on the cross turned out to be the turning point in history, when reconciliation with God was made possible. And in the ultimate plot-twist, Jesus rises from the dead. Behind every happy ending lies this Christian story. Have you ever wondered if all this affects us so profoundly, not merely because it's emotive, but because it's actually true?

4

Have you ever wondered why humans are attracted to the supernatural?

Gareth Black

As a child I was a huge fan of the TV series *The X-Files*. Every week I would avidly tune in to follow FBI Special Agents Mulder and Scully on their next investigation into those classified, unsolved cases of paranormal activity. The character dynamics of the show's two protagonists is fascinating. Fox Mulder readily believes in the existence of aliens and the paranormal. He's convinced that *'the truth is out there'* despite the best efforts of corrupt authorities to cover it up. By contrast, his partner Dana Scully is a sceptic, a woman of science assigned to empirically scrutinise Mulder's work by offering rational explanations for the phenomena they encounter.

Fast-forward to today and our fascination with the supernatural continues apace: dramas like *Stranger Things*, *Charmed*, or *The Rings of Power* dominate the viewing figures. In 2021 the gambling organisation *888Poker* revealed that three in every four Britons consider themselves to be superstitious. And so, despite the apparent decline of public interest in 'organised religion', belief in God and life-after-death, together with self-help spiritualities, remain hardy perennials of human interest.

What is it about humanity that leads so many of us, across time and cultures, to be natural-born supernaturalists? Three centuries beyond the scientific enlightenment, many of us retain an unshakeable, Mulder-esque curiosity for the paranormal that confounds our Scully-like naturalistic better judgements. *Have you ever wondered why humans are so attracted to the supernatural and the spiritual?*

Sceptical scientist and author of *The Believing Brain*, Michael Shermer, argues that the reason is found in our cognitive psychology. Supernatural beliefs are simply a vestige of two concepts left over from our evolutionary heritage: *'patternicity'* which Shermer defines as 'the human tendency to find meaningful patterns in meaningless noise', and *'agenticity'*—our tendency to believe that the world is controlled by invisible, intentional agents. Shermer writes:

> *The problem is that we did not evolve a baloney-detection device in our brains to discriminate between true and false patterns. So we make two types of errors: a type I error, or false positive, is believing a pattern is real when it is not; a type II error, or false negative, is not believing a pattern is real when it is. If you believe that the rustle in the grass is a dangerous predator*

when it is just the wind (a type I error), you are more likely to survive than if you believe that the rustle in the grass is just the wind when it is a dangerous predator (a type II error). Because the cost of making a type I error is less than the cost of making a type II error and because there is no time for careful deliberation between patternicities in the split-second world of predator-prey interactions, natural selection would have favored those animals most likely to assume that all patterns are real.[1]

In a similar vein, Christopher French, professor of psychology and head of the Anomalistic Psychology Research Centre at Goldsmiths, University of London, suggests that we often believe in the supernatural because of the emotional crutch it offers us against the horror of oblivion: 'The vast majority of us don't like the idea of our own mortality. Even though we find the idea of ghosts and spirits scary, in a wider context, they provide evidence for the survival of the soul.'[2]

The problem, however, with explanations such as French and Shermer's is that they are merely *interpreting* longings for God or the supernatural through a presupposed naturalistic framework. For them, paranormal phenomena can only *ever be* our evolutionary psychology playing tricks on us because they have already decided that the supernatural does not exist. All Shermer and French offer is an explanation for why we might believe in the supernatural in the context of an exclusively natural universe.

But what if supernatural phenomena aren't delusions but signs of an ultimate reality beyond that physical universe? In that case, Shermer's materialistic explanation of supernatural belief could simply be a direct product of his own *'anti-patternicity'* or *'anti-agency'*. And couldn't *dis-belief* in the supernatural prove as useful a psychological crutch as faith? For, as Aldous Huxley once admitted regarding the basis for his scepticism: 'I had motives for not wanting the world to have a meaning; consequently assumed that it had none, and was able without any difficulty to find reasons for this assumption.'[3]

But what if our supernatural intuitions are not simply the inconvenient, delusional residue of evolution? What if, rather than quickly dismiss them because they don't fit with our materialist assumptions, we might allow them to raise serious questions about whether a materialist worldview is the right one after all?

After all, it is only within a world that operates according to regularities (such as the laws of science) that we would be able to identify the presence of irregularities intervening from the outside. We see this in fiction—it is only *because* characters live in a world where things don't fly off shelves or go bump in the night by themselves that they can identify the presence of supernatural agency. This, of course, doesn't mean that every creak in the house is caused by a monster under the bed. Rather, it is simply to suggest that perhaps we shouldn't dismiss supernatural claims quite so hastily.

Perhaps the truth really is *out there* whether, like Mulder, we want to believe or, like Scully, we don't. And if *the truth is out there* then perhaps we have a responsibility to investigate it. Of course, if we suspect that the truth out there might be the kind of hideous, malevolent creature committed to our destruction then we may have good reasons for remaining agnostic. But what if the opposite is the case? What if, like the character Murph in Christopher Nolan's film *Interstellar*, we discover that *behind* the supernatural phenomena confronting us is a benevolent being; a being whose primary purpose in breaking into our world is to communicate information that ultimately leads to our salvation?

5

Have you ever wondered why we crave money despite knowing it's not the answer?

Andy Moore

As we stumble through financial turndowns and cost-of-living crises, many in our society are contemplating financial decisions which might seem more appropriate in a Charles Dickens novel. For some, the choice has come between putting food on the table and heating our homes. Recessions are a recurring part of our national life, plus personal financial issues can hit even when the wider economy is doing well. It's frightening and we think that if we could just have a little more money, then all our problems would be solved. In these uncertain times, many of us instinctively try to build a healthy bank balance in search of a healthy sense of security.

I don't claim to be any different. When the economy in the UK took a nosedive in 2020 and I felt the financial pinch, we started renting out the spare room in our house and took on extra work to earn more money. But at the same time I know, as I think we all do, that money in the end won't make me happy. So have you ever wondered why we crave money despite knowing it's not the ultimate answer? Surely there's something deeper, more real, more satisfying, more reliable, and better at the heart of reality than the fleeting security that money provides?

Since ancient days, humanity has wondered where lasting happiness can truly be found. One book, above all, has shaped the trajectory of Western philosophy—Aristotle's *Nicomachean Ethics* written around 400 BC. In a work of several hundred pages, Aristotle starts with one thought which he takes to be fundamental to the understanding of the human pursuit of happiness: we do and seek things according to what we think will result from those actions. This reveals a hierarchy of purposes and motivations which link all the way up to the one thing we regard as more important than anything else.

We do X because we think Y will result, and then upon having Y, Z becomes possible and so on. Maybe the reason we want food on the table is so we can work. Work earns us money, so then we can buy a house, a house becomes a home, a home allows us raise a family and so on. That seems like pretty sound logic. But then, says Aristotle, if there is something we wish for because of itself, and not because it leads to something else, and if all the other things we want lead up to this end goal, then this will be our chief good. He writes:

> *If we could know it, it would have great significance. Like archers with a target we would be so much more successful in hitting the point if we had this knowledge.*[1]

Unfortunately for Aristotle, this is where he came unstuck. He never worked out what that thing could be, that thing which might be an ultimately worthy pursuit, a genuine source of happiness and security (though that didn't stop him waffling on for many more pages!).

Fast-forward a few centuries to Jerusalem and along comes Jesus of Nazareth with his answer. Jesus doesn't need thousands of pages of turgid philosophy, but rather spoke with an authority all his own when he said:

> ... *do not worry about your life, what you will eat or drink; or about your body, what you will wear. Is not life more than food, and the body more than clothes? ... But seek first his kingdom and his righteousness, and [to paraphrase] everything else starts to make sense under that.*[2]

In the trenches of day-to-day life we often find it impossible to keep focused on the right things. When we're in survival mode, worried that we might lose our job or distracted by umpteen other preoccupations, we construct security using pieces of a jigsaw which only add up to a picture reflecting *this* world: paying the mortgage, job security, husband, wife, children, girlfriend, boyfriend, sport, the environment, charitable causes, degrees and qualifications, status in society, and so forth. These things are important—but we need to look through and beyond them to see where we really ought to be seeking our happiness and placing our security.

Perhaps the good things we experience in our lives on earth are meant to be enjoyed, even as we recognise they are always incomplete. They capture our imaginations like a letter from a loved one far away, or a brochure for a home that will soon be ours. That home, according to Jesus, is the 'Kingdom of God' and there is more than just the material world around us—for 'life is more than food'.

Sometimes it feels as if God is absent, or if he is there, he's got no interest in our lives. Especially in difficult times. Yet according to Jesus, our Heavenly Father is committed to providing for us, and when our relationship with him is in the ultimate position, that's when things start to make sense. I wonder if you know that to be true? If there's nothing in your bank account, where else will you look? We often crave money despite knowing it's not the answer. So in these crazy times, might it be worth seeking God first?

6

―――――

Have you ever wondered why we are drawn to beauty?

Mary Jo Sharp

I spent my childhood years in the beautiful Pacific Northwest of the United States. My parents loved the outdoors and we frequently took family trips to see the mighty Pacific Ocean or the majestic volcanic peaks of the Cascade Range. I loved to sit quietly, revelling in the overwhelming beauty I encountered. Although as a child it was difficult to put into words, I knew beauty meant something and that it was something good.

Over time, I began to wonder what all this beauty in the world was for and why it has an undeniable draw on us human beings. The nature shows I watched said the spectacular beauty in the animal kingdom was explained by an instinctual preference to preserve a species. However, the sheer vastness of the beauty around us—Mozart symphonies, a Van Gogh masterpiece, the sunset on the ocean—seemed to be ridiculously beyond what was instinctually necessary to attract a mate. I sensed that beauty pointed me towards something higher, deeper, and everlasting, not just something physical and immediate.

In my senior year of high school, a music teacher whom I greatly respected caught me at just the right moment when I was searching for some answers, such as the meaning behind beauty, and gave me the gift of a Bible. As I thumbed its pages, I came across these words:

> *One thing have I asked of the LORD,*
> *that will I seek after:*
> *that I may dwell in the house of the LORD*
> *all the days of my life,*
> *to gaze upon the beauty of the LORD*
> *and to inquire in his temple.*[1]

Though I had never thought about it before, I began to ponder the idea that God might be beautiful. I reasoned that if there was some kind of Creator, and if he made his creation in reflection of his own qualities, then perhaps the beauty in creation is intended to draw me towards him, in the same way as a great piece of art draws me to know the artist.

However, it's not just the splendour of the natural world that has such sway, it's the beauty of humans as well. I sometimes wonder if we have difficulty encountering the pull of God's transcendent beauty because we've forgotten how truly beautiful humans are. I'm not simply referencing physical beauty, but also the design of the human body, the emotional depth, cognitive complexity, moral quality, plus the unity in diversity we exhibit. If nature's beauty strikes a chord with us, then humanity is an entire symphony of experiences. And that symphony ignites our desire to understand who and what we are as human beings, calling to us that we are so much more than a cosmic accident.

The timeless quality and irreplaceable value we see in each other are not best explained as arising from chance and matter with no aim or end. Such origins would leave these attributes void of proper meaning, and give us no apt reason for why we should even comprehend them at such depth. By way of analogy, chaotic origins would seem to reflect the indifference of John Cage's composition *4:33* in which music is defined as anything and nothing, rather than the meaning-packed complexity of Tchaikovsky's *Swan Lake*, in which there is masterful musical form and purposeful emotional intent.[2] Our human attributes similarly entail intentionality, purpose, and worth; qualities that arise from an artist, a personal Creator, rather than from unconscious forces.

There is an aesthetic of meaning and value to our lives, and we're attracted to it just like we are attracted to beauty and design in nature. Humans are an irreplaceable work of art that compels us to discover the artist behind it all.

Not only does beauty serve as a signpost towards the Creator, the ever-increasing discoveries of science aid our understanding of how beauty impacts our mental health and wellness as well.[3] Combinations of colour and light, as well as their outworking in art, can improve human psychological wellbeing, resulting in astounding effects such as quicker recovery from illness.[4] Furthermore, studies have found that humans respond positively to scenes of nature and to spending time surrounded by natural beauty:

Over 100 studies have shown that being in nature, living near nature, or even viewing nature in paintings and videos can have positive impacts on our brains, bodies, feelings, thought processes, and social interactions. In particular, viewing nature seems to be inherently rewarding, producing a cascade of positive emotions and calming our nervous systems.[5]

Beauty impacts us and calls to us in every aspect of life. From our mental and physical health to our greater understanding of what it means to be human, we are constantly faced with the aesthetic of meaning and intentionality, the beauty of design. Essentially, our experiences of beauty point us beyond the immediate and subjective towards recognising something transcendent and objectively beautiful, the Creator God. The desire for beauty in our everyday lives finds its ultimate fulfilment in him, for we have been made by a perfectly beautiful Artist.

7

Have you ever wondered why we hate selfishness and admire altruism?

Andy Bannister

One of my favourite stories is Charles Dickens' classic novel, *A Christmas Carol*. We recently had the joy of introducing our children to arguably the definitive version, namely, *The Muppet Christmas Carol*. I have little doubt that as Dickens scribbled away in 1843 on his novel, he clearly had Kermit the Frog, Miss Piggy, and the rest of the muppet menagerie in mind.

If you're unfamiliar with *A Christmas Carol*, it tells the story of Ebenezer Scrooge, an utterly mean, miserly, selfish old man. But as he is confronted by the ghost of his former business partner, Jacob Marley, followed by the spirits of Christmas Past, Christmas Present, and Christmas Yet to Come, Scrooge undergoes a transformation and becomes a generous, kind, and charitable soul.

The story works because it taps into one of our core assumptions: namely that meanness is wicked and charity is commendable.

Dickens could assume that his audience instinctively knew that Scrooge 1.0 should be booed, and Scrooge 2.0 should be cheered. If your reaction to *A Christmas Carol* is to regret the transformation and miss the old miser of act 1, you're a bit of a moral muppet.

It's not just in fiction that we sneer at the selfish and admire the altruistic. I recently read the account of Billy McFadzean, a twenty-year-old soldier who, in 1916, was fighting in the trenches of World War I. A box of hand grenades slipped into a crowded trench, dislodging the safety pins of two of them. Realising what was about to happen, McFadzean threw himself on top of the grenades, which exploded, killing him, but his action saved the lives of dozens of his comrades. Billy was posthumously awarded the Victoria Cross.[1]

I had no sooner read that story than I turned on the news and discovered that the celebrity Kim Kardashian was being lambasted on social media because she had apparently gone to a friend's birthday party and taken it as an opportunity to hog the limelight by snapping lots of photos of herself, leaving her friend stuck in the background of her own party. Twitter was aflame with condemning hashtags and #SoSelfish was trending.

Whether it's fact or fiction, our gut reaction is selfishness, *boo*! Selflessness, *hoorah*!

But why is it that we admire altruism? What is it about somebody helping another person, often at great cost to themselves, that we find so deeply attractive? Why is it that when we catch ourselves behaving selfishly (snaffling all the cookies; refusing to share; hoarding our resources, time or talents) we feel guilty, knowing deep down that we *should* do better? Why beat ourselves up in this way?

If we live in a purely material universe, our feelings don't make sense. If this life is all there is and evolution is the only game in town, then what, frankly, is wrong with selfishness? Indeed, more than that, aren't we wired to be selfish? The Oxford atheist and biologist, Richard Dawkins, titled his famous book on evolution *The Selfish Gene* to make this very point. As he puts it bluntly:

> *We are survival machines—robot vehicles blindly programmed to preserve the selfish molecules known as genes.*[2]

It shouldn't take a rocket scientist (or even a biologist!) to see the problem here. On this logic, if Dawkins were to see an old lady unrelated to him drowning in a river, he could cry 'No benefit for my genes here!' and walk by. No problem. Yet I suspect the next day's newspaper headlines would *not* be, 'Selfish Genes Saved as Scientist Lets Granny Sink'.

Deep down, we all know that biology is not humanity's only story. Indeed, trying to explain human nature purely in terms of our genes is as wooden as saying 'music is merely a series of noises', '*A Christmas Carol* is just a string of letters', or 'Kim Kardashian is simply some carbon, water, iron, calcium, phosphorous and iron'.

Maybe another of Dickens' novels, *A Tale of Two Cities*, can help us here. In that story we read about two characters, Charles Darnay and Sydney Carton, who look almost identical. They both fall in love with the same woman, Lucie Manette. Lucie chooses Charles; they get married and have a child together. The novel is set during the French Revolution and Charles, a French aristocrat, is arrested and sentenced to execution by guillotine.

On the night before the execution Sydney visits Charles in prison. Since they look alike, Sydney suggests they swap places, thus allowing Charles to escape. Charles refuses but Sydney has him drugged, smuggled out of the prison, and then whisked away safely to England along with Lucie and their child.

That night in the prison, a young seamstress who has also been condemned to death comes to speak to Sydney, assuming him to be Charles Darnay. Suddenly she realises the switch and, astonished, she whispers in awe: 'Are you dying for him?'

'And his wife and child. Hush!' replies Sydney.[3]

Where does that theme of self-sacrifice come from? It comes from the Bible, a book Dickens knew well. It's the theme at the heart of the New Testament where Jesus gave his life in our place—'This is how we know what love is: Jesus Christ laid down his life for us.'[4]

If we live in a godless universe, self-sacrifice and other acts of altruism are cute, but ultimately deluded. If our selfish genes are pulling our strings, then he who dies with the most toys (or the most genetic descendants) has won the lottery of life. If we live in that kind of universe, we should be celebrating selfishness and ridiculing altruism. But I would suggest that the fact we are horrified by this thought is a significant clue that we're living in a very different kind of universe.

Our problem comes when we realise that although we value altruism highly, we're not always very good at living it out. As much as we enjoy and are inspired by stories such as *A Christmas Carol* and *A Tale of Two Cities,* they often don't result in lasting change—they might *move* us, but they can't *change* us; they lack the power to do that. However, at the heart of the Christian faith lies the claim that the story of the ultimate act of altruism, Jesus sacrificing his perfect life for our broken lives, is not intended merely to be inspirational; rather it is a story, a *true* story, that—if we respond to it—offers far more than just motivation. It offers us the power to change.

8

Have you ever wondered why the environment matters?

Andy Steiger

'Do you care about the environment?' This has become a defining question of the twenty-first century, one that we find ourselves continually answering indirectly in the daily decisions of our lives. I was once asked this question directly. As I walked out of a bookstore, I was greeted on the street corner by a friendly college student wearing a Greenpeace t-shirt and holding a clipboard. He was delighted to hear that I *did* care about the environment. He explained to me how people are destroying the planet but that I could do something about it by making a donation. Before I opened my wallet to support this worthy cause, I wanted to pursue the question deeper. With genuine interest, I asked: '*Why* should I care about the environment?' It was obvious from his silence and blank stare that I had identified something of a cultural blind spot. After pondering my question for a while, he responded: 'We should care about the environment for future generations.'

The answer 'future generations' is one of the most common responses I hear from those questioned about why they reduce, reuse, and recycle. It's not a bad answer in so far as it goes, but notice this logic is established on the value of people not nature. Intuitively we understand that we don't owe a rock anything, even one the size of a planet. This is because one's moral duty is owed to persons not things. It's why we walk on rocks and not people.

Unfortunately, some individuals have taken our moral duty to protect the environment to an extreme. For example, both New Zealand and Canada have granted legal personhood status to rivers. Before this piece of innovative aquatic law-making, New Zealand had already made legal precedent by giving personhood status to a forested hill country called Te Urewera, a piece of land that now technically owns itself. These legal moves grant these rivers and land the same value and rights as a human person. Although I appreciate this was done to protect the environment for future generations, it undermines its own project by calling into question the unique value of people.

We must remember that after WWII, the Universal Declaration of Human Rights was created to stop people from ever being devalued again. That document begins with the now famous declaration that all humans have inherent dignity. *Inherent* means that our value is encountered not created. That is, we come into the world with value. No human gave it to us, and thus no human can legitimately take it away. Our desire to protect the environment for future generations gives voice to that shared dignity we encounter in each other. However, when governments begin giving the same value to an object or an animal, it cheapens, and even undermines, our own dignity; it is the very definition of dehumanising. Similar to poor environmental stewardship, future generations will pay for the mismanagement of our human value.

Is it possible to find a basis for saying 'the environment really matters' without that statement depending on us? Here again, we quickly run into the problem that things only matter or have value in relationship to a person or persons. This is where modern philosophy presents a very depressing perspective—by devaluing people, it continues to undermine environmentalism. For example, Alex Rosenberg, the chair of the philosophy department at Duke University, succinctly summarises the foundation of modern thinking: 'The physical facts fix all the facts.'[1] This seems to sum up the secular perspective and leads philosophers, such as Rosenberg, to the following conclusions: *'What is the nature of reality?* What physics says it is. *What is the purpose of the universe?* There is none. *What is the meaning of life?* Ditto.'[2]

I expressed my concern over this physics-only worldview with the man from Greenpeace by asking: 'Why bother caring for the environment or future generations?' He looked perplexed, so I offered an explanation: 'Physics tells me that the sun is dying and as it does it will expand until the earth is consumed in fire. If my life and the planet are destined for destruction and are ultimately meaningless, I might as well get what I can while I can.' With a mix of profanities, he said, 'That's messed up.'

'I agree,' I told him, 'but why?'

I find it odd that so many universities today teach that the physical facts fix all the facts and yet you should still recycle.

What do I owe a meaningless universe? Nothing! In which case we can kiss goodbye to environmentalism. If that seems a bit bleak, is there an alternative? Perhaps we need to rethink our worldview. Perhaps we know the environment matters with or without us because our planet exists in relationship to another person—the Creator God.

My own answer to why the environment and future generations matter is because God matters. As a follower of Jesus, my responsibility to the environment and future generations is grounded in my relationship to God, who gives life and the universe meaning, purpose, and value. If you care about the environment and future generations, I encourage you to invite the person of God into your thinking.

9

Have you ever wondered why mathematics works?

Andy Bannister

Maths is everywhere. Even if the phrase 'let's do some maths' seems as exciting as 'let's take up stamp collecting' or 'how about a wet weekend in Bognor Regis?', you can't escape the fact that all of us use maths, dozens of times a day. Whenever you ride a bike, make a budget, bake, cook, or catch a ball, maths is involved—whether you're using it or not!

We simply can't get through life without numbers, especially when it comes to science. For example, when NASA launched the James Webb Space Telescope to international excitement in December 2021, there was a lot of maths involved in ensuring it got to the right place, at the right time, and pointed the right way. Whether it's launching a space probe, modelling the curvature of space-time, or calculating orbital trajectories, scientists are utterly reliant on mathematics.

This is because nature is inherently mathematical; numbers are written into the laws of physics and mathematical patterns turn up everywhere. For example, in AD 1202 the Italian mathematician Leonardo Bonacci, more popularly known as Fibonacci, described a series of numbers like this:

1, 1, 2, 3, 5, 8, 13, 21, 34 ...

Each number in the series is the sum of the two numbers before it. And it's a pattern that turns up all over nature: the Fibonacci Sequence describes the growth of animal populations, the number of petals on flowers, the spirals on a shell and so forth. It also turns up in aesthetics, with the Fibonacci Spiral popping up all over art and architecture. This connection led the atheist philosopher, Bertrand Russell, to remark, 'Mathematics, rightly viewed, possesses not only truth, but supreme beauty.'[1]

But why does maths work? Numbers are all around us, so we don't tend to stop and think about them—but it's incredible that life, the universe, and everything seems to align so well with mathematics.

Here's the problem. If we live in a purely material universe, where the ultimate reality is atoms and particles, then what actually is a number? What *is* '2'? I mean you can't sit on it, lick it, or whack it with a hammer. Instead, numbers are a human invention, a creation of our minds. But if numbers are merely objects of human thought, then how is it that numbers also describe the very fundamental building blocks of the universe? Mathematical constructions—from numbers like '2' to concepts like 'i'[2]—turn up all over nature. As Professor Jim Al-Khalili, former president of the British Humanist Society, put it:

It's a huge philosophical question: Why does nature speak the language of mathematics?[3]

Furthermore, numbers and maths seem to be really real: something that mathematicians discover, not something they invent. There isn't 'Chinese maths', 'British maths', or 'Indian maths'—there's just *maths*. Mathematical concepts don't change depending on who discovers them, they're universal. But how can mental constructions like numbers exist outside of human minds? What *is* going on?

In 1960, the Hungarian physicist Eugene Wigner published a now famous essay, 'The Unreasonable Effectiveness of Mathematics in the Natural Sciences', in which he explored this conundrum. Wigner begins with the story of two friends, one of whom was a statistician working on population trends. The statistician showed his friend an essay he was writing which included a mathematical equation concerned with population growth on the first page. 'What's this little π symbol here?' the friend asks. 'Oh, that's pi, the ratio of a circle to its diameter?' 'You're having a laugh,' his friend retorts, 'what on earth has the population to do with the circumferences of circles!'[4]

Wigner goes on to show how, repeatedly, mathematics and science (whether it's demographics or physics) fit together like a hand in a glove. Wigner admits that scientists cannot explain *why*, but that nevertheless we should be extremely grateful that they do. He concludes:

The miracle of the appropriateness of the language of mathematics for the formulation of the laws of physics is a wonderful gift which we neither understand nor deserve. We

should be grateful for it and hope that it will remain valid in
future research and that it will extend, for better or for worse,
to our pleasure, even though perhaps also to our bafflement, to
wide branches of learning.[5]

Numbers can do a lot. But there are some things that numbers can't do—they can't, for example, solve bigger questions like telling us the value of a person, the purpose of existence, or the meaning of life. Hence why attempts to reduce the whole of life to that which can be indexed, measured, or numerated reminds me of an episode from Douglas Adams' novel, *The Hitchhiker's Guide to the Galaxy*. A group of scientists have built a super-computer, Deep Thought, tasked with answering the question of the meaning of life. After seven and a half million years of contemplation, Deep Thought is finally ready to announce the final definitive answer to the Great Question of Life, the Universe and Everything:

'You're really not going to like it,' observed Deep Thought.

'Tell us!'

'Alright,' said Deep Thought. 'The Answer to the Great Question ... Of Life, the Universe and Everything ...'

'Yes ... !'

'Is,' said Deep Thought, and paused. ...

'Yes ... !'

'Forty-two,' said Deep Thought, with infinite majesty and calm.

It was a long time before anyone spoke. Out of the corner

of his eye Phouchg could see the sea of tense expectant faces down in the square outside.

'We're going to get lynched aren't we?' he whispered.[6]

When it's later suggested to Deep Thought that the answer is somewhat anti-climactic, the computer retorts that it's likely nobody knew what the question actually *was* with any precision.

Numbers cannot tell us the meaning of life. But numbers might be a *clue* as to where that meaning is located. For if nature is fundamentally mathematical then it seems that whatever the deepest level of reality is, we're looking at something more like a mind, rather than mere atoms and particles. Which is, fascinatingly, precisely what the Bible has always claimed: in the beginning, it says, was not a molecule, nor an atom, nor a field of quantum particles, but God himself, the ultimate mind, in which numbers and mathematics have their source.

10

Have you ever wondered why music has the power to move us?

Michael Ots

Imagine for a moment, if you can, a world without music. Imagine a film with no soundtrack; a wedding where the bride walks into the church in complete silence; or a Six Nations rugby match where the anthems are simply spoken rather than sung.

In one sense life could continue perfectly well without music. The storyline of the film would be unaffected. The couple would still get married. The game would still be played.

Yet in a deeper way we would have lost something precious. While the soundtrack to a film is not something we are always consciously aware of, it plays a huge part in helping us to 'feel' the impact of what we are seeing. The music accompanying a bride's entrance deepens the beauty and solemnity of the moment. And as for singing the anthems ... I'm sure that for the Welsh rugby team at least, the sound of 80,000 of your compatriots singing the anthem is worth at least a ten-point head start!

Music is powerful. It can stir emotions, awaken desires, and instil courage. Music is so important to us, but have you ever wondered where it comes from?

If life is simply the result of the evolutionary process (and nothing more) as many atheists believe, then accounting for the beauty of music is problematic. The atheist philosopher Patricia Churchland expressed her view of life this way:

> *The principle chore of nervous systems is to get the body parts where they should be in order that the organism may survive ... a fancier style of representing [the world] is advantageous so long as it is geared to the organism's way of life and enhances the organism's chance of survival.*[1]

In such a view a thing is only really good in as much as it helps us survive. But does music exist simply to enhance our chances of survival? Perhaps, for instance, the ability to create music might make you more attractive to a potential mate? Perhaps that would explain why lots of my friends learnt the guitar during our teenage years?!

Yet, like so many evolutionary explanations, while this may explain why *some* people might make *some* music, it seems a fairly poor explanation for everything from Bach to Bon Jovi. And while this line of argument may satisfy some, it doesn't convince many musicians. I was recently chatting to a friend who, like myself, works in universities across the country. She commented that while they've met many atheists studying many different things, she were yet to find one who was studying music. I'm not saying that there aren't therefore *any* musicians who are atheists but, anecdotally at least, it would seem there aren't so *many*. Why is this the case?

In conversation with thousands of students, one common reason I've heard people give for why they *don't* believe in God is the presence of so much evil and suffering in the world. How can God exist in a world that seems at times to be so utterly futile? This is a good question and worth exploring.[2]

But if the presence of so much ugliness in the world turns us away from the idea of God, what do we do with beauty when we stumble across it? Music seems to have a way of tearing us away from the mundane futility of life and confronting us with more.

This happened to me on a school trip to London many years ago. I can't remember the main purpose of the trip but I do recall very distinctly a moment in Covent Garden at the end of the day. We happened to walk past a string quartet just as they started to play Pachelbel's 'Canon in D'. I had never heard the piece before but I remember being struck by the incredible beauty of the music as it filled the air. The bustle of the passing shoppers seemed to diminish as I became enraptured by what I was hearing.

Without a word being spoken I had somehow been reminded, even in the midst of a busy market, that there is real beauty in this world. It's a memory I will never forget.

The author and philosopher C.S. Lewis also spoke about how a childhood experience of beauty spoke to him powerfully later in life. He was, until his 30s, an atheist, and one of his main reasons for not believing in God was the unnecessary suffering he saw in the world. Yet for Lewis, the memory of that experience of unnecessary beauty haunted him. That moment had created a deep sense of joy which he found hard to shake. It was this experience of beauty and the joy it produced, that became one of the main influences in him eventually embracing the Christian faith. He later wrote about this experience in his book *Surprised by Joy*.

Could the beauty of music awaken us to our desire for something beyond what we can see, touch and even hear? Could our experiences of beauty be, as Lewis wrote elsewhere, 'the scent of a flower we have not found, the echo of a tune we have not heard, news from a country we have never yet visited'.[3]

It seems that beauty experienced through music has a way of challenging even the most sceptical to reconsider their view of the world. The philosopher Paul Gould explains how music has been doing that in Japan. In a country that has traditionally been unreceptive to the claims of the Christian faith, he explains that the music of Johann Sebastian Bach now plays a key role in drawing people in the country to take a deeper look at Jesus. Gould explains why:

> *The beauty [of Bach] has prompted the Japanese to ask: How can Bach exist in a world full of despair and loneliness? Answering the question has set several Japanese people on the path to Jesus, who is the source of Bach's inspiration and the source of beauty itself.*[4]

Yet, you might ask, why do we need to bring God into it? Can't we just be thankful to the composers who created such music? But do we really just create music or do we in some sense also discover it? As I child I loved to create things with Lego (OK, I'll admit it—I sometimes still do!). But I didn't *create* Lego, rather I simply worked with the pieces that had already been made. In a similar sense it seems that this might be what we are doing with music—working with what we have already been given to create something beautiful. I wonder if within the beauty of the music lies an invitation to discover not just the genius of the composer or artist, but also the ultimate composer and artist that stands behind it all?

11

Have you ever wondered why humans are so incurably curious?

Mary Jo Sharp

My father loved cosmology. He often shared with me his wonder at the vastness and complexity of the universe. I recall an occasion when I was about twelve when he woke me in the middle of the night to watch a meteor shower from our back porch. He fetched two lounge chairs and some blankets, and together we watched the incredible display as the bright, burning rocks soared through the night sky. I asked my father, 'What do you think is out there?' He replied, 'I don't know, but it's fascinating, isn't it?'

We humans are incredibly curious creatures. As soon as we begin to talk, we immediately start asking, 'Why?' We want to know how and why things work. We investigate and discover the existence of things. We marvel at creation. This intellectual curiosity has driven humanity to make impressive discoveries about our world and the wider universe, and has advanced technology in every conceivable field.

And curiosity is not just something that happens inside our heads. We share thoughts and ideas with others, testing out our knowledge and expanding our depth of understanding. This often leads to friendships and relationships and further exploration of ideas, which, in turn, builds community.

But why are humans so curious? Is there anything we can say about the origin of our inquisitive nature? Is it explainable simply in material terms—the accidental offshoot of our genetic programming to survive and reproduce, or is it a clue to something bigger?

In one of the oldest parts of the Hebrew Bible, we find some intriguing words: God creates humanity 'in his own image'.[1] When God brought humanity into existence, we were created to mirror something of God himself, and one way we reflect this is through our rationality and self-awareness. Those gifts, wired deeply into our nature, drive our curiosity and passion to ask questions about *everything*: from the world around us, to ourselves, to questions about God and spirituality.

With our inbuilt wonder and curiosity comes a sense of humility. As I sat in that lounge chair and watched the meteor show with my father, I remember being struck by a feeling of wonder at the *immensity* of the universe; and even as a twelve-year-old, I realised that if we are alone in the universe, just an accidental arrangement of atoms, we really are deeply and truly insignificant.

If there is a loving God behind everything, that not only gives us a ground for our sense of wonder and a basis for humility at our place in the scheme of things—but it does so in a way that doesn't crush us with a sense of hopeless insignificance. We can acknowledge ourselves to be just one tiny person in a vast universe *and yet* know we are valuable. As it says elsewhere in the Hebrew Bible:

> 'For my thoughts are not your thoughts, neither are your ways my ways,' declares the LORD. 'As the heavens are higher than the earth, so are my ways higher than your ways and my thoughts than your thoughts.'[2]

If humans could fully comprehend everything about God, then I would argue that God is obviously something of our own creation. However, if there is a God who created the universe, including humans, then I would expect him to be greater than us in every way. But at the same time, knowing this God chose to create us reflecting something of his nature must mean that we are far more than a '1% bit of pollution in the universe' as atheist cosmologist Lawrence M. Krauss once memorably dismissed human beings.[3]

Have you ever wondered why humans are so incurably curious? Why we have this urge to discover what's over the next hill, the next horizon, or in the neighbouring galaxy? It's hard to make sense of if we are just the product of the random forces of time and chance. But *if* there is a bigger story, then perhaps your sense of wonder is a clue to the God who made you in his image and wired you for curiosity.

Wondering is a mechanism through which we grow and mature. It helps us to be ever inquisitive about ourselves and our world. It also helps to remind us of our intellectual position in the universe; not just of *having* knowledge, but also recognising that we *lack* knowledge. And as we begin to understand the things that God has made, perhaps we begin to understand something about this Creator God.

My father helped to cultivate in me a lifelong love of discovery and learning. And that is what we humans were made to do: to seek out information about ourselves, our world, and our Creator. We were made for a relationship with the awesome and infinite Creator God, the source of our insatiably curious minds.

12

Have you ever wondered why black lives matter?

Clare Williams

The question, 'Why do black lives matter?' seems redundant because surely it is self-evident that everyone, regardless of ethnicity, is worthy of life. Our shared humanity is enough to answer this provocative question. And yet, there is clearly something prompting the inquiry, 'Why do black lives matter?' Our common humanity, and the fact that 'all lives matter' is indeed true, but is there something about the way our society operates which gives the impression that black lives don't, in fact, matter?

Often when we are confronted by the problem of racism in the UK, we can be quick to point a condemnatory finger at the US or some other part of the world, because we believe the issue isn't that bad here. However, some disturbing statistics suggest we should be alarmed. Black women are four times more likely to die in childbirth than white women.[1] Black children are more likely to be strip-searched by police.[2] Black Caribbean children are more likely to be permanently excluded from schools.[3] And by their own reporting, police use greater force with black and Asian suspects than white suspects.[4]

Growing up black in Britain, I remember my parents telling me that I would have to work twice as hard as my white peers to be taken seriously. I remember my dad telling me how to conduct myself if I ever got stopped by police; he had been stopped several times, including one time on his way to church! I remember teachers scoffing at my ambition to apply to Oxford University and saying, 'You'll only get in because of positive discrimination.' While teaching in multicultural London schools, I remember going over and above in my duties to show that black women could lead well. But all of this hard work didn't stop white colleagues who struggled with their own classes telling me, 'The kids listen to you because you're black.'

The thing is, working twice as hard does help to overcome some barriers but it's incredibly exhausting. It is a relentless cycle of seeking worth from individuals and systems that set a higher bar for faces that don't fit. And this is not to disregard disadvantages which people experience because of class. Not at all. During my years of teaching, I have seen the struggle of white working-class boys in education and the research which highlights their particular situation.[5] Since leaving teaching, I have set up a charity which supports them and other underrepresented groups in aspiring to higher education.[6] However, I am also keenly aware that racism compounds class disadvantage.

Even if we're not convinced that racism is the main cause

of disparities for ethnic minorities, we must admit that there is something much deeper to consider: what are the implications of a society in which black people must prove they're worthy of being treated with dignity, that their lives matter? If black lives only matter if they perform well or we measure worth by what individuals contribute to society, we are setting everyone up for failure. Why? Because this kind of metric turns us all into objects which can be used, rather than people with inherent dignity. Regardless of ethnicity, we will all face limitations when we age, get sick, lose our jobs or some other tragedy strikes. Do our lives cease to matter then?

I have been alive and black for 36 years, and I can tell you that this type of thinking doesn't work. It's dehumanising to both black and white lives. How so? In his strident narrative denouncing nineteenth-century slavery, Frederick Douglass describes how slave-buyers came to inspect him and other enslaved Africans in a prison. He writes:

> *A swarm of imps, in human shape the slave-traders, deputy slave-traders, and agents of slave-traders ... watching for chances to buy human flesh (as buzzards to eat carrion) flocked in upon us ... Such a set of debased and villainous creatures, I never saw before, and hope never to see again.*[7]

The objectification of Africans in this scene is horrific *and* it also reveals how the slave-buyers were dehumanising themselves with this behaviour. Something of our humanity is lost when a person views someone else as a thing or a product. When someone exploits others, slowly and surely their sense of respect for the dignity of people becomes warped.

Christianity subverts this idea completely. Firstly, human dignity is grounded upon the claim that we are made in God's image.[8] Like a Banksy is worth more than a painting by someone just starting out, the value of the art is ultimately determined by the acclaim of the artist. In the same way, Christianity says that we are God's masterpiece, and he delights in us, painting a diverse palette of people across the globe.[9] My life matters, not because of achievements or when others think I've done enough as a black person. I matter because in my very blackness, I reflect something of God himself.

Secondly, the Christian faith is hinged upon the concept of grace. Getting to know God is not about the things *we* can do but about what *he* has done for us. We can't earn our way into relationship with God. Our skin colour cannot give us special privileges or access to God. Instead, Christianity is the great leveller, for it says that we are all broken and in need of a saviour—and that is exactly who Jesus claimed to be.[10]

13

Have you ever wondered why we find loneliness so difficult?

Michael Ots

I have never been more alone. I was paddling my canoe down the Whanganui River in New Zealand, and since pushing off from the bank five days earlier, I had been totally on my own. The steep wooded valley sides ensured that I had no phone reception for the duration of the journey. Yet to this day this remains one of the happiest experiences of my life. I was alone, yet never once did I feel lonely. Conversely some of my loneliest moments in life have been when I was surrounded by others: a crowded college, a busy restaurant, a packed music festival. So, what actually *is* loneliness, and why do we find it so difficult?

We might assume that loneliness is an age-old problem, but it's not, at least not according to cultural historian Fay Bound Alberti. In her fascinating book, *A Biography of Loneliness,* she explains that the concept of loneliness, in its modern negative sense, didn't really exist in the English language before about 1800.[1] It's not that people were never alone before that, but their experience wasn't perceived negatively in the way that it is now.

So, what is making us so lonely? It would be easy to lay all the blame on social media, and it's certainly not without its problems—watching an endless feed of carefully curated highlights from other people's lives can certainly compound our feelings of loneliness. However, the modern problem of loneliness predates the invention of the internet.

Fay Bound Alberti suggests two reasons for our modern experience of loneliness. Firstly, the popular appropriation of Darwin's theory of evolution profoundly changed the way we view other people. In a world where only the fittest survive, it is all too easy to go from seeing other people as community and instead view them as competition. We can't all succeed, so our success depends upon someone else's failure.

Secondly, the decline of religious belief in the West has changed how we view being alone. Alberti explains that up until 1800 it was more common to describe the state of being on one's own as 'solitude'. However, unlike loneliness, solitude was seen as a positive thing. While solitude means being cut off (for a time) from human connections, this was normally done with the intention of developing one's connection with God. The French mathematician Blaise Pascal once remarked, 'All of humanity's problems stem from man's inability to sit quietly in a room alone.' Pascal himself had come to experience this profound connection with God that enabled him to see time alone not negatively as a loneliness, but positively as a solitude.

Have you ever wondered if one problem of living life without any thought of God is that when we are alone, we really are alone with no one else to turn to? And perhaps this means that we end up seeking the kind of love, belonging, and intimacy from others that we were actually meant to get from God himself? Our disappointment in others may, at least partly, be because we are asking too much of them. What if we were designed to connect on the deepest level with the Creator of the universe? No friend, neighbour, colleague, lover or even spouse will be able to fill that void.

If it is the case that we were created to connect, not just with each other, but also with God himself, how might we rediscover that connection? How could it become a personal experience and not just an abstract concept?

In her moving novel, *Beautiful World, Where Are You?*, Sally Rooney's four main characters provide a profound reflection on the challenges of living in contemporary society. All of them are seeking connection and belonging in world that has left them feeling both alone and adrift. One of the characters, Alice, despite her suspicion of institutional religion and her fear of appearing weird, finds herself being drawn to consider afresh the person of Jesus—not just a character from literature or even just a historical figure, but as someone that she could actually love in a meaningful sense.

As I consider the accounts of Jesus's life, I'm struck by the fact that although he is often alone (a deliberate decision to enable him to experience solitude with his heavenly Father) there is only one occasion when he seems to experience what we might call 'loneliness'. During his crucifixion, Jesus is abandoned—not just by his friends and followers, but seemingly by God himself. The Christian contention is that Jesus, who knew the deepest connection with God, somehow gave up that connection so that we might gain it. Through Jesus's disconnection we can find reconnection with God himself.

14

Have you ever wondered why we treat sex as something sacred?

Anne Witton

We live in an age obsessed with sex. It's at the heart of TV shows like *Sex in the City*, *The L Word*, *Sex Education*, *Love Island*, and *Heartstopper*. Scandals about the illicit romantic liaisons of the rich and famous always make the headlines and boost ratings. For years advertisers have cynically used sex to flog cars, perfumes, and even bread. Sex sells. Magazine problem pages and online forums are full of sexual angst. Are we getting enough? Too much? Are we doing it right? How can we improve our performance?

But have you wondered why we idolise, worship, and obsess over sex to such an extent that it has become the god of our age? And why—if sex is venerated so much—we also cheapen it by having one-night-stands and meaningless encounters, treating it like a simple bodily function akin to eating a chocolate bar? As the secular feminist Louise Perry remarks:

> *Liberal feminism incorporates sexual disenchantment as an article of faith, insisting that it is a good thing that sex is now regarded as without inherent value in the post-sexual revolution era. But, in practice, liberal feminist women do not generally behave as if they believe in the truth of sexual disenchantment. Almost no one does.*[1]

Our relationship with sex is complicated, but most people spend a considerable amount of time thinking about it and worrying about it even if they're not doing it. Most of us have an instinctive desire to be found sexually attractive. It seems that we often look to sex to complete us and validate us. We even call our sexual partners our 'other half'. We seek sexual fulfilment to prove that we matter and are beautiful or handsome. It gives us confidence and makes us feel loved. Sometimes it makes us feel macho, powerful, and in control. We often want to have sex so that we don't feel we're missing out. We want to feel desired.

Our twenty-first-century culture isn't unique in idolising sex. A quick survey of ancient Greco-Roman art and literature highlights the array of erotic practices that were widespread in those civilisations. We may think that we live in the most sexually liberated era, but, as the writer of the book Ecclesiastes in the Bible wryly put it: 'there is nothing new under the sun'.[2]

In some ways, this obsession is natural. After all, none of us would be here if it wasn't for people having sex. But unfortunately, so often it doesn't deliver what it promises. Sex can bring about a great amount of pleasure, but it can also cause a huge amount of pain and disappointment, especially when we use it selfishly or expect it to perform a role it was never designed for.

The reality is that the sexual revolution of the 1960s and 1970s—which promised more sex and better sex for all—hasn't delivered. Surveys vary, but the pattern is consistent. We're having sex (at any age) on average three times every four weeks when in previous decades it was five.[3] Half of women aged 25–34 don't enjoy sex.[4] Half! National libido is in decline. Sexual satisfaction is in decline. Over just six years, the number of people who rated themselves as good at sex dropped from 55% to 33%.[5] The average number of sexual partners a person has in a lifetime has gone up,[6] yet Nicholas Wolfinger, a sociologist at the Institute of Family Studies, observes that the evidence suggests the more sexual partners you've had, the less satisfying you find sex.[7] It seems like the reality for many people doesn't match the marketing and Hollywood glitz.

As humans, we all need intimacy. We're made for deep connection. We long to be completely known and unconditionally loved, and yet many of us look for that love in human sexual relationships that will ultimately disappoint us. Marriages end, people have affairs, sex can be painful or disappointing. Even in the best romantic relationships, one partner will die before the other. Sex is often great but it can never deliver *everything* we expect or hope from it. So is there any good news or are we doomed to chase a satisfaction that is always just out of our reach?

People often think that Christianity is squeamish about sex or that it's incredibly restrictive because God is some kind of cosmic killjoy. In fact, the opposite is true. There's a whole book of the Bible (Song of Songs) that graphically and poetically depicts the joy of a sexual relationship between two lovers. God made sex as a beautiful and enjoyable thing. There is something so powerful in the act of sex. It fuses together two souls in a moment of ecstasy and unity.

But here's the even better news for all of us, whether we're in a sexual relationship or not. Sex is just a reflection of something bigger and even more profound. Sex points beyond itself to the exquisite joyful union that we can all experience for ever with the God who made us and loves us intimately. It is a very deliberate picture of the depth of relationship that God wants to enjoy with anyone who will turn to him. We are loved and wanted and we don't need a sexual relationship to experience that. Only Jesus can meet our deepest desire for intimacy, for love, to be fully known. So we can confidently look forward to experiencing an eternity enjoying the full depth of God's love, but we don't have to grit our teeth in the meantime. A deeply satisfying and rich relationship that meets all our deepest needs and longings is available to us right now. As the Bible puts it:

> ... *as a bridegroom rejoices over his bride, so will your God rejoice over you.*[8]

Jesus came to bring us the greatest possible connection that will ultimately satisfy, so why not continue to explore God's heart for you by exploring Christianity with thought and care.

15

Have you ever wondered what love is?

Gareth Black

Our culture is fixated with love and romance. We're told that love always wins, and if you can find love, find that perfect relationship, everything will be wonderful. This is a message reinforced by movies, TV shows, and songs—all of which repeatedly proclaim that it's through true love that all our hopes will be fulfilled. As The Beatles famously sang, 'All You Need Is Love'.

The capacity to love and be loved is arguably the most universal human characteristic. Its presence transcends every boundary of time and culture. Love has been the inspiration for, or a constituent theme of, almost all of the greatest works of literature, music, and art that the world has ever produced. It's central to many religious and ethical movements. And the personal experience of knowing love is such a universal human desire, that the promise of finding it has generated the billion-dollar match-making industry.

But have you ever wondered what *love* actually is? It's a much harder question than our familiarity with the word might suggest. Indeed, the word 'love' is thrown around so casually in our culture that its meaning is in danger of becoming lost, or at least watered down. We talk of loving our jobs, our pets, our phones, our hobbies, our houses, our cars, even our sports teams. Modern tautologies like 'love is love' don't help us much either—what does it mean for 'love' to be 'love' unless we first know what love means?

Were we to ask a neuroscientist, we might be told that love is simply brain chemistry; merely a result of the behaviour of the vast assembly of nerve cells and associated molecules impacting our hormone levels, as the atheist biologist Francis Crick asserted. But is love really just an illusory product of our biochemistry, a cruel trick played on us by our genes in order to drive us to reproduce?

Such reductionist conceptions of love won't work for romantics. After all, when was the last time you bought a Valentine's card for your beloved and penned the inscription: 'When I think of you my brain causes a disturbance which I feel in my gastrointestinal region'? Or: 'Roses are red, violets are blue, my selfish genes deterministically led me to you'? Instead, we prefer to understand love in terms of the powerful attractions, ethereal emotions, and deep joy we experience when we look into another's eyes. Yet the danger with this sentimental deification of love is that when such emotions fail, so too does the love with which we have conflated them. As Margaret Atwood lamented in *The Handmaid's Tale*:

God is love, they once said, but we reversed that, and love, like heaven, was always just around the corner ... We were waiting, always, for the incarnation. That word, made flesh.[1]

Like Atwood many of us recognise that if love means anything, it has to be more than mere words or an abstract concept: it has to be 'made flesh'. The interesting thing is that many of the most profound and enduring things written about love, come from individuals who believed that God is love and that love has been personified in Jesus Christ. It was Jesus, incidentally, who said something remarkably insightful about love:

Greater love has no one than this: to lay down one's life for one's friends.[2]

I find it fascinating that everybody *instinctively* knows that Jesus was right. From the most pious religious person (of whatever faith) to the most dogmatic secularist, we all know, deep down, that there is something very special going on when one person gives their life for another. Whether it's a fictional story in literature, or when we hear a news report of a parent giving their life for a child, dying to save another shows us what love is.

I recently read an account of the engineers on the *Titanic* who didn't run to the lifeboats as the boat started to sink, but stayed below decks, keeping the engines running and the lights on, to facilitate the rescue of as many passengers as possible. Although they went down with the ship and paid for their gallantry with their lives, they are still recalled as heroes today, over a hundred years later. Laying down one's life for others is seen as the epitome of goodness.[3]

Stories like these move us deeply, because we know in the very fibre of our being that this type of love is incredibly impressive. Real love is not cheap, true love is costly, and the highest form of love is self-sacrifice, love that is willing to expend itself for another, even at the price of one's own life.

But Jesus didn't merely offer a helpful thought on the subject of love, he also put those words into action. At the heart of the Christian faith stands the belief that Jesus, no mere man but God-with-us, gave his life when he went to the cross to deal with our rebellion, self-centredness, pride, greed, and apathy. As it says elsewhere in the New Testament:

> *God* demonstrates *his own love for us in this: while we still sinners, Christ died for us.*[4]

If Jesus was who he claimed to be—God come in the flesh, God stepping into space and time, getting his feet dirty with the dust of the earth and his hands bloody with the nails of the world— then what we see in Jesus's willingness to go to the cross, to deal with our brokenness and our mess and our hang-ups, is the greatest possible act of love by the greatest possible being. He loved us so much, even while we were his enemies, that he was willing to do that.

Have you ever wondered if your life is worthwhile?

Clare Williams

Scrolling through social media, we swim daily in a sea of memes, motivations, and messages which millions of people use to affirm their lives. Find something inspiring? Like and share. Find something triggering? Block and delete. But the question of our worth cannot be answered simply by our daily diet of feel-good digital content. It is a deeply confronting question because it demands that we examine our standard for a life well lived. Have you ever really stopped and wondered what is the measure of a worthwhile life?

There are three common ways in which we attempt to answer this question: success, self-care, and selflessness. Let's start with the first. *Success*. A good education, a well-paid job, a loving partner, 2.4 children and a healthy body seem to be self-evident indicators of a great life. Education demonstrates that we've worked hard; a top job that we've worked harder. A partner and progeny show that we're loved and that we haven't been rejected—that we're doing well at the game of life. But what happens if we don't make the grade? What happens if we're made redundant, our loved ones pass away, or our health is compromised? Does the loss of these things (and they are very good things too) mean a loss or decline in the value of our lives? Surely not.

When we discover that a *successful* exterior life can't truly satisfy, sometimes instead we look within and try *self-care*. We recite positive affirmations, practise gratitude, detox, and diet. Our mood improves and we face life's challenges with a renewed sense of purpose. Self-care is healthy and healing for many of us. And yet, the reality is we don't always feel good about ourselves. We don't always eat clean and workout dirty. We don't always have something profound to say when life gets hard. Does a dip in our personal wellbeing and inner peace therefore undermine the value of our lives? Again, surely not!

So rather than looking within, sometimes we opt for looking outwards and trying *selflessness*. We redirect our focus and energies onto the needs of others. We pour ourselves into our families. We volunteer. We stand with the marginalised and give to the less fortunate. We campaign and call for justice. Genuinely seeking out the liberation of others is a beautiful act. Doing the work of justice is a rewarding and exhausting pursuit. Such self-sacrifice has undoubtedly been instrumental in the moral progress we have made over millennia. But can we ever reach perfection? It seems there will always be a cause for which to contend. And who takes care of the heroes? It's impossible to always be saving the day; we must take some time to put down our capes.

Perhaps success, self-care, selflessness, or a combination of all three will always be found wanting. So, should we stop taking ourselves so seriously and simply throw out the idea of a worthwhile life altogether?

In the final movie of the *Jurassic Park* trilogy, a young and brilliant scientist reflects upon the age of the earth and the dinosaurs which traversed it long before humans ever did. She muses that the very idea of a planet billions of years old and the existence of species much stronger and fiercer than our own should humble us. Perhaps she's right—instead of looking for success or looking within or without, should we look back and bask in the wonder of our insignificance? Simply acknowledge that we are tiny specks in the expanse of time, creatures of spectacular mediocrity? This view is not just the stuff of fiction.

In his essay, 'Sanctity of Life or Quality of Life?', atheist philosopher Peter Singer asks a chilling question:

> *Why should we believe that the mere fact that a being is a member of the species* Homo Sapiens *endows its life with some unique almost infinite value?* [1]

In this vein, there is nothing about being human that legitimises any presumption of the intrinsic worth of ourselves or our lives. While it's possible to subscribe to this view intellectually, can we do so *practically*? Is it liveable? In the day-to-day grind of joys and injustices, even Peter Singer behaves as if *his* family have value; we all act as though the good things that come our way are deserved and bad things are unfair, precisely because we intuitively believe we're people of worth. And what if this intuition is correct, and not just a fuzzy feeling?

Moreover, success, self-care, and our attempts at selflessness also fail to deliver a lasting sense of worth because of their impermanence. They're fleeting. They're not sustainable. They're only parts of a story that (if Peter Singer's atheism is true) comes to an abrupt and unfulfilling end. However, the Christian worldview tells a different story. We are encouraged not merely to look back, within, or without, but to look up. To look to a God who has created us with inherent dignity and value because we are made in his image. As the African-American public theologian Ekemini Uwan writes:

> The image of God, also known as the imago Dei, is not a supplementary gift or addendum, nor is it accidental. The imago Dei is irrevocable.[2]

So when we fail, when we feel we're not enough, when we can't cure the ills of this world, and when we feel insignificant, we can look up. We look up to a God who has stepped down into human history in the person of Jesus and affirmed our lives as worthwhile.

17

Have you ever wondered why we preserve the past?

Anne Witton

I have a box under my bed full of objects which hold special memories for me. It contains letters and photos, a champagne cork, a little plastic gun, a lip balm, some beads, a temporary tattoo, a golf tee—all reminders of special moments from my past. Maybe you have something similar. It's important to many of us to preserve a record of our past. We erect gravestones after loved ones have died and we pass heirlooms down through the generations. But have you ever wondered why?

We also put a lot of time, effort, and money into preserving our collective past. History and heritage are a national pre-occupation. England alone saw 20 million visitors to English Heritage sites in 2022, plus more than 5.3 million visitors to National Trust properties.[1] The National Trust for Scotland welcomes 3 million each year to their properties, and Historic

Environment Scotland a further 1.2 million.[2] Meanwhile, the British Library keeps a copy of every publication produced in the UK and Ireland and has 13.5 million books in its archives, covering everything from Cicero to Chomsky.[3] But again, why are we so keen to preserve the past?

One reason is often to build on the knowledge and insights of those who have gone before. Scientific discoveries and technological advancements rarely come out of the blue. They're usually the result of great minds developing ideas of others. As Isaac Newton once said: 'If I have seen further, it is by standing on the shoulders of giants.' We also hope to avoid disaster by learning from the errors of others. Tim Harford's excellent podcast *Cautionary Tales* examines past mistakes and farces to equip us with insight into how we can do things differently in the future.[4] We ignore the past at our peril, as George Santayana famously remarked: 'Those who cannot remember the past are condemned to repeat it.'

A less utilitarian reason for preserving the past is to value communities and cultures. We want to recognise the worth of traditions, diversity, and creativity, for example by not letting minority languages like Welsh or Gaelic languages die out, nor by allowing heritage crafts like woodturning to become a lost art.

But I do wonder whether the main reason we preserve the past is to get a sense of who we are and where we belong in the world. The popularity of TV programmes like *Who Do You Think You Are?* and websites like ancestry.co.uk reveal our desire to understand the bigger story of our families and communities. We want to know where we fit, perhaps to give us some insight into our character, our destiny, and the meaning of our lives. To truly know who we are, we know we need to understand the past, which shows us where we've come from and reveals the bigger perspective of our lives. Appreciating the past gives us a context to understand our present and future.

And what if there's an even bigger story that we're all part of? Remembrance and preserving the past are deeply significant in the Christian tradition. The Bible itself is a historic book that has been read more than any other on the planet. It has been translated in full into over 700 languages[5] and there are thousands of preserved manuscripts of the New Testament.[6] The Bible's importance has been recognised around the world throughout generations.[7]

The Bible gives us a valuable insight into a historic drama that is continuing today. Re-enacting the past was crucial for the Israelite people, a highlight being the annual Passover festival which celebrated God's rescue of his people from slavery in Egypt. It is still celebrated by Jews (and some Christians) today, as a way of remembering God's faithfulness, love, and care for his people. This historic event points to the unchanging character of the timeless God.

Jesus celebrated a Passover meal with his closest friends just before he went to the cross to die for all of us rebels and make a way for us to come back to God. He used the bread and wine as symbols for his body and his blood, communicating the profound truth that he would sacrifice himself to mend the rift between us and God:

> *[Jesus] took bread, gave thanks and broke it, and gave it to them, saying, 'This is my body given for you; do this in remembrance of me.'*[8]

Christians continue to remember this historic event, rehearsing the story of their origins, how they got here, and how this reminds them of their identity and God's character. It gives Christians strength for the future.

If Jesus was on *Who Do You Think You Are?* the researchers wouldn't have a very difficult job as two of the historical biographies in the New Testament contain Jesus's family tree, tracing his ancestry right back to Abraham, the father of the people of Israel. Jesus wasn't just parachuted into a random moment in history. The whole unfolding of Old Testament events was leading up to his coming, which has profoundly shaped human knowledge, endeavour, communities, and lives ever since.

Personal, community, and cultural memorabilia, from gravestones and precious family photos to museums and national monuments, help us to preserve the memory of things that are important. We rightly dread the thought that things this precious might one day be merely dust; gone, forgotten, and remembered by no one. Christian faith brings something distinctive to this aspect of the human condition. Many religious systems in the ancient world used sacrifices to try and manipulate the gods to bless everything from homes, to crops, to relationships—in other words to gain leverage over the gods to get them to participate in *our* story. The Christian faith says the opposite: that in Jesus, God sacrificed himself so that we could be part of *his* eternal story, a story in which every moment, memory, thread of hair on our heads, and fibre of our being is redeemed and saved for eternity.

If all we have to hope for is that our future descendants might remember us, we'll probably soon be forgotten. (Do you remember your great-grandparents?) But if the Christian story of reality is true, then we can know *now* that we can have a hope for the *future* because of what God has done in the *past*.

18

Have you ever wondered who you really are?

Michael Ots

The story is told of a couple of lads who stumbled out of a pub one night having had a bit too much to drink. As they staggered down the road trying to find their way home, they came across a very smart, uniformed, naval officer. One of the lads called out: 'Oi, mate, do you know where we are?' Somewhat offended by their rather over-friendly approach, the officer looked down his nose at them and declared: 'Do you know who I am?'

At this the lad turned to his mate and exclaimed: 'Now we're really in trouble. We don't know where we are, and this bloke doesn't know who he is!'

Have you ever wondered 'Who am I?' or 'What makes me, me?' The way we answer that question usually depends on the culture we live in.

Non-western cultures (and previous generations in the West)

would commonly say that the answer to that question is external to ourselves. We need to look outwards and listen to who society tells us we are. In such a culture our identity is something given to us by our family and society.

A good example of this are the surnames in the English language. Why are some people called Cook or Smith or Baker and so on? Clearly, at some point these names were descriptive of the family profession. In such a society a certain set of expectations were placed upon you from birth. Your vocation and other life choices were given to you.

There are some benefits to such a way of doing things. Life is much simpler, and in some vocations, passing skills down through the generations can be highly beneficial. But it is also very restrictive. What if I don't want to be a cook or a gardener like my father before me? What if my own personality, desires and natural abilities don't fit the expectations laid upon me?

Today in the West most people would answer the question 'Who am I?' in a very different way. Instead of looking out to see what other people say, we are encouraged to look in and find the answer in our own desires and feelings. Our identity is not something given to us but something we can choose. We feel that we should be free to create our own identity, and that no one else should be able to tell us who we are.

In some ways this is a very liberating mindset. We are no longer restricted by cultural expectations and stereotypes. For instance, when people first discover my wife works for an airline, many automatically assume she is cabin crew and are very surprised to discover she is actually a pilot. (Passengers have been known to ask her for drinks as she walks to the flight deck!) It's great that her career hasn't been limited by those expectations and that she has been free to choose and pursue her childhood dream.

However, is it really true that I can be *whoever* I want to be? When I was a child, I discovered I was flat-footed and needed special insoles in my shoes. The main result of this was that I wasn't very good at running. Therefore, no matter how much I might have desired to be an Olympic hundred-metre champion, that dream was never going to be realised. The limitations of our own physicality will, at least in part, determine who we are (and aren't).

We also need to consider whether it is wise to refuse to listen to others, and to only consider our inner, subjective sense of self. Couldn't others help me discover who I am and what I am good at (or not)? Imagine for instance that I decide to be a great comedian. The only issue is that no one ever finds me funny! How do I respond? I could try ignoring people's opinions and pressing on with my attempted career. But before long, I'd probably be telling jokes only to myself. And this goes much farther than career choices. We are constantly refining our sense of identity based on the reaction of others.

We should also ask whether we are really as free as we think we are? We laugh at previous generations and their conformity to a set of societal expectations. But are we really more free today, or are we just conforming to a different set of expectations? Just look at what happens when people question some of those expectations on social media. The debates around free speech, self-censorship, and 'cancel-culture' suggest that we are not as free as we think we are.

Both looking out to society and looking inwardly to our desires can have *some* value in helping us find out who we really are. But what if our identity was not simply something given to us (from outside) or something we chose for ourselves (from within), but rather something to be discovered?

One ancient Hebrew poet expressed it this way when he wrote: 'I am fearfully and wonderfully made'.[1] The poet didn't view himself simply as the result of biology and sociology, but as the creation of a loving God.

If this were true then it would mean we have a value and significance inherent in who are, and not just because of what we do. We are, after all, human *beings* not human *doings*! In fact, the Christian faith says that God loves and values us deeply not based on what we do, but in spite of what we do! He is a God who loves us even with our screw ups, brokenness, and failings, and is willing to forgive us (at great cost to himself).

If we truly are 'fearfully and wonderfully made' it also would mean your uniqueness is not simply the result of random chance but of design. Could it be that God has created you with a unique combination of abilities, desires, and interests? If this is the case then maybe our identity is not something we chose but rather something to be *discovered*. The joy of the Christian faith is that I don't have to build my identity all by myself, nor even simply conform to the expectations of those around me. We can get to know the God who created us in a personal way. In relationship with him, we can discover who he created us to be and how we can use that to make a difference in this world.

19

Have you ever wondered why suffering and evil seem so wrong?

David Nixon

Several years ago my wife and I returned home from a Christmas concert, full of festive fun and cheer. As we descended the steps to our basement flat, something didn't seem right. I had left the outside light on—but it was switched off. The front door was slightly ajar. Cautiously I entered the flat to find that we had been burgled. The thieves had been through everything—every drawer, every cupboard, every room!

I remember two distinct feelings at that moment. First, it was unspeakably cold because for hours the flat had been drained of heat and flooded with the cold winter air. I also remember my intense reaction: 'This is wrong!'

That feeling of *wrongness* is worth considering further. It wasn't just that I wished it had never happened. After all, who among us wants to have our lives touched by evil? Of course we don't want to have a loved one taken away from us by age or disease, to lose a job or income, or to suffer an injury or accident. However, my reaction was not merely, 'I don't like this', reducing it to the category of personal opinions such as 'I don't like Marmite'. But rather, 'This is morally wrong. The world *ought* not to be this way!'

But why? Although all living creatures in this world experience suffering, only humans perceive it as a *moral* problem, not just a fact of nature. Secularism struggles to make sense of this intuitive experience. For example, the scientist Richard Dawkins says:

> *In a universe of blind physical forces and genetic replication, some people are going to get hurt, other people are going to get lucky, and you won't find any rhyme or reason to it, nor any justice. The universe that we observe has precisely the properties we should expect if there is, at bottom, no design, no purpose, no evil, no good, nothing but pitiless indifference.*[1]

Yet, when bad things happen to us, we don't greet them with 'pitiless indifference'. We feel wronged; we know things shouldn't be this way; we want justice.

I would argue we instinctively know we live in a moral universe with moral laws and standards. And more than that, there is no moral law apart from a law-giver. This was the realisation of the former atheist and Oxford University professor, C.S. Lewis:

> *My argument against God [when I was an atheist] was that the universe seemed so cruel and unjust. But how had I got this idea of just and unjust? A man does not call a line crooked unless he has some idea of a straight line.*[2]

The problem of suffering itself implies the existence of God. Nevertheless, you might question what kind of God would allow us to suffer.

When we look at the world and when we experience its brokenness, we are not seeing the world as God intended it to be in the beginning, nor as God plans to restore it in the end. Rather we find ourselves in the middle of this story. But the good news is that God has not remained distant and unfeeling from our pain. Instead, in an act of incredible love, God has sought us, coming into this world to rescue us, in his Son, Jesus. God has walked many miles in our shoes, he has worn our skin, he has felt our pain, he has drunk the same bitter cup of suffering. The author Tim Keller puts it well when he says:

> *Christianity alone among the world religions claims that God became uniquely and fully human in Jesus Christ and therefore knows first-hand despair, rejection, loneliness, poverty, bereavement, torture and imprisonment.*[3]

The surprising claim of the Christian faith is that God did that because he loves you so much! Jesus came not just to sympathise with us but to save us. And he did it in this surprising way: Jesus became an innocent victim of evil in order to vanquish it. In so doing he has made it possible for us to be reconciled with God and rescued from evil that lurks within us and around us in this world.

History records that Jesus not only died as a victim of evil, but that he rose again three days later as our champion over evil.[4] The tyranny of evil has its days numbered, its greatest weapons have proved impotent against God. The resurrection of Jesus assures us that there is coming a day when our longings will be satisfied: good will triumph over evil, death will die, tears will cease, and pain will be healed. Just as Jesus's body was raised from the dead, so that is the pattern for our broken bodies and our broken world. Restoration is coming.

What are we to do about suffering until then? That's a question explored by the Russian novelist Fyodor Dostoevsky. In his celebrated book *The Brothers Karamazov*, we are introduced to Ivan the atheist and Alyosha the Christian. Ivan is a sceptic, deeply troubled by the suffering of innocent children in the world. He cannot intellectually understand how a good God could allow such things to happen, so reluctantly rejects God. Ivan attacks his brother's faith, posing some of the most difficult philosophical questions against all that I've shared with you in this chapter. Alyosha is unable intellectually to answer all of Ivan's questions—instead he kisses his brother and then goes and befriends a group of impoverished street children, seeking to help make their hard lives better and alleviate their suffering. In doing so Alyosha is following in the footsteps of Jesus and showing what we can do, even if we don't have all our intellectual questions answered in this lifetime.

So the next time you find yourself suffering and saying, 'This seems so wrong', you're right—it is! But at that moment, allow this feeling to lift your mind and heart to God in heaven, and be reminded that he does care—because Jesus shows that he does—and he will act to put things right.

20

Have you ever wondered why we long for justice?

Clare Williams

During a recent binge-watching marathon, I stumbled upon *Don't Look Up!* a Netflix satire, which points an irreverent, accusatory finger at celebrity culture, big tech, government, social media trends, conspiracy theories, and everything else supposedly wrong with the world.

At the end of the film, one of the more villainous characters meets an absurd and violent end. (Don't worry, no spoilers!) As I watched the character's farcical fate, I was strangely pleased. Although the means of their demise was outlandish, it didn't mean that it was undeserved. The narcissist finally got their comeuppance and, as I sat in the sofa seat of judgement garbed in my onesie, my wrath was appeased.

But life is not a movie. The injustices we experience are far weightier matters than the plot of a film. There's no pause or fast-forward button to get to the best bits and, no matter how angry we are about some of the ways we've been treated, there is no rewind button. Our inability to control what happens to us makes our longing for justice even more poignant.

But why do we long for justice? If our existence is the outworking of impersonal cosmic forces, if we are nothing more than biochemical machines, why do we petition, picket, and protest for justice? Someone might argue our activism is pre-determined by the whims of a mindless universe. Or maybe our longing for justice is just an illusion, an evolutionary instinct for the survival of our tribe. Perhaps our calls for justice can be explained simply as virtue-signalling coming from a desire to look good.

I think these conclusions are too cynical. Many of us genuinely care about the suffering of others. We make an autonomous choice to speak up and out for marginalised voices. When the whole world was struggling to breathe, coming face to face with its own mortality due to the coronavirus, many of us were deeply moved by the horrific death of George Floyd as he cried out, 'I can't breathe!' But why did seeing this spark global protests?

In her powerful book, *Where is God in all the Suffering?*, Amy Orr-Ewing writes:

> *Whether we believe in God or not, whoever we are, we are creatures of dignity. If that is true, the essential part of you that makes you you has a transcendent source. Your value is not imagined or invented—it is real, and its grounding is God's image in you.*[1]

Unlike the cold, silent universe which cannot bestow value upon any of us, the Christian faith talks about a God who has given every member of the human family inestimable worth because we are all made in his image.

We each sense that people are valuable and justice should therefore be carried out for all. When we say 'That's not fair!' or 'They shouldn't be able to get away with that!' we are appealing to an objective standard of justice and proclaiming that others *should* agree with us. We believe that others *should* see that our cry for justice is legitimate. But if nothing is at the root of human existence, where does our sense of something—our belief that we have value and worth—come from? Without a Creator God, our desire for justice makes little sense.

But while we are often quick to be vocal about what others deserve, what do we do when we find the accusatory finger of justice pointing at us? When it turns out that maybe it is *we* who have acted unjustly? Suddenly we desire the benefit of the doubt. A second chance. Mercy. If we're honest, perhaps we wouldn't survive our own standards of justice. We are ready to lower the gavel of our own morality metric upon others, but expect clemency when we ourselves are in the dock.

The words of poetry from the Hebrew Bible make our predicament clear:

> ... *justice is far from us,*
> *and righteousness does not reach us.*
> *We look for light, but all is darkness;*
> *for brightness, but we walk in deep shadows.*
> *Like the blind we grope along the wall,*
> *feeling our way like people without eyes.*[2]

Our longing for justice is a good, legitimate desire. And yet it prosecutes us even as we grope for it in the dark. We can't attain the very standard we seek and apply to others. Yet the good news of the Christian faith is that Jesus, the Wholly Just One, has come near to us. He has reached out to us. He has brought light and sight. Unlike our fleeting, subjective standards of justice, Christianity points us to a person within whom all justice ultimately resides—Jesus. The Bible promises that one day, he will put all things right.

Our longings for justice are not imagined, hopeless, or meaningless. So next time you find yourself crying out for justice—whether for yourself or for others—wonder for a moment about what that longing for justice says about you, the universe, and reality. This might just be a clue towards the compelling prospect of a God who gives us a basis for desiring all wrongs are put right.

21

Have you ever wondered what happens when you die?

Anne Witton

Growing up, I found death both fascinating and terrifying. Knowing what happened after death felt essential for finding purpose and meaning in life. After all, if death negated everything I've spent my life investing in, was it really worth doing anything at all? It would be like spending years crafting a wonderful novel, only to set it on fire when it's finished. If the only meaning to life is enjoying the moment and 'Being in the present, the here and now is the ultimate reward of life',[1] then what's the point in existence for all the billions of people globally whose lives are full of suffering and hardship? My question was, in the words of the Russian novelist Leo Tolstoy:

What will come of what I am doing today or shall do tomorrow? What will come of my whole life? ... Why should

I live, why wish for anything, or do anything? … Is there any meaning in my life that the inevitable death awaiting me does not destroy?' [2]

How about you? Have you ever wondered what happens when you die? Are we just a bunch of random atoms that will be rearranged into something else when we snuff it? Do we just cease to exist or will we perhaps be reincarnated as someone or something else? Do we have an eternal soul that will survive our physical death? Will we face judgement? Is there hope of a life to come or do we simply live on in the memories of the generations that come after us? If the passing on of our genetic material is our legacy, where does that leave the millions of people who don't have children? Whatever you believe happens when you die, it seems a pretty significant question to wrestle with.

The sad reality is that most of us will be completely forgotten in a couple of generations. According to a recent YouGov survey, just seven percent of Brits expect to be remembered for more than 50 years after their death. [3] Even people who have made a significant contribution to human history often only have the sketchiest facts associated with them after a few hundred years. For instance, William Shakespeare is one of the most famous people who ever lived, but what do we actually know about him? We don't know what he would be like to talk to. We don't know what he really cared about or who his best friends were. Some people have even tried to contest his authorship of all the plays attributed to him! [4]

With many of us increasingly living our lives online and sharing more and more information digitally, we now leave much bigger footprints behind us, but the question is: who is going to go looking for all this in a couple of generations? Most of us—however notable in our culture's eyes—will be completely forgotten, even by our own families. Each generation gets diluted; we have two parents, four grandparents, eight great-grandparents and so on. Even at the stage of great-great-grandparents you've got sixteen people you probably know very little about, just four generations removed. That's how transient and ephemeral life is unless it's given some kind of transcendent meaning.

The book of Ecclesiastes in the Bible highlights well the ultimate futility of life if God is removed from the equation:

> 'Meaningless! Meaningless!'
> says the Teacher.
> 'Utterly meaningless!
> Everything is meaningless.'
> What do people gain from all their labours
> at which they toil under the sun?
> Generations come and generations go,
> but the earth remains for ever ...
> No one remembers the former generations,
> and even those yet to come
> will not be remembered
> by those who follow them.[5]

So where can any of us find ultimate meaning? Many look for the answer in spirituality and religion. Most religions teach that there is some kind of afterlife, whether that is reincarnation, rebirth, or resurrection. The concepts of heaven and hell are known but widely misunderstood today. We have a vague sense that good people go to heaven and bad people go to hell. Yet the message of Christianity is radically different from any other faith (and from what you might expect). It teaches that none of us *deserve* to go to heaven (as we've all messed up). But the good news is that Jesus has paid the price for our brokenness and rebellion against God through his death and resurrection. Because Jesus was raised from the dead,[6] it guarantees that anyone who puts their trust in him can enjoy an everlasting life as it's meant to be, free from suffering, evil, and pain.[7]

This is at the heart of what Christianity is all about and what, for me, gives ultimate hope to life. Jesus teaches about having the right priorities in life—living for the eternal rather than just the temporary. He counsels us to invest in that which won't be rendered void by the inevitability of death, and to work for that which lasts:

> *Do not store up for yourselves treasures on earth, where moths and vermin destroy, and where thieves break in and steal. But store up for yourselves treasures in heaven, where moths and vermin do not destroy, and where thieves do not break in and steal. For where your treasure is, there your heart will be also.*[8]

If we put our trust in Jesus, there is the promise of an inheritance which can't fade or be destroyed, but will instead last for ever. We will enjoy eternal life with him and all the goodness of a restored creation, restored relationships, and a new body long after our bodily death here on earth. Whether you're afraid, nervous, or simply unsure about your mortality and death, that's surely a promise worth investigating.

22

Have you ever wondered if you're a good or a bad person?

Andy Bannister

Most of us want others to think well of us. We want to believe that our friends, neighbours, and colleagues consider us decent people, not that they secretly think we're untrustworthy or obnoxious. We hope that when our backs are turned, people are singing our praises, instead of warning others not to come within a mile of us.

This natural desire for people to think well of us is why we work hard at being nice, friendly, and polite. It explains the rise of virtue signalling (ensuring that our friends know that we support all the correct causes and are on The Right Side of History™). And it's the reason many of us carefully polish our social media feeds, so that the digital shop window to our souls gives the right impression. As the journalist Stephen Marche put it: 'Curating the exhibition of the self has become a 24/7 occupation.'[1]

One reason we do this is because we live in an increasingly judgemental society, with forgiveness a long-forgotten virtue. The nineteenth-century atheist, Friedrich Nietzsche, predicted the rise of societies where, although the concept of God had all but been rejected, religious ideas like judgement would be retained (just shorn of any notion of forgiveness or redemption). That prediction describes our twenty-first-century world well; and so ensuring people think we are *good* is just basic self-preservation.

But have you ever wondered if there's more to being a good person than that? Most of us, I suspect, like to imagine that were we offered the chance to do something wicked with absolutely no chance of getting caught (steal a million pounds, cheat on a loved one, kick an annoying puppy, buy a Justin Bieber album), we wouldn't do it. We like to believe that our decency is more than just performative.

But can we be sure? After all, modern history shows how normal human beings can be truly monstrous given the right circumstances: many of the atrocities of the Third Reich, for example, were carried out by ordinary people who would go home to their families each evening after a day of torturing and murdering. As the film director Stanley Kubrick once commented, talking about his movie *The Shining*:

> *There's something inherently wrong with the human personality. There's an evil side to it. One of the things that horror stories can do is to show us the archetypes of the unconscious; we can see the dark side without having to confront it directly.*[2]

Or think of it this way: if an app was invented that allowed anybody to see every thought you've ever had, every word you've ever uttered, and every deed you've ever done—how many of us would give the login code to our friends? To our spouse or partner? To our beloved 83-year-old grandmother? There may not be a grinning Jack Nicholson lurking in our personal shadows, but there are probably a few skeletons.

Can you really know if, overall, you're a *good* person or a *bad* person?

One way might be to decide for yourself. Get up in the morning, look in the mirror, stand up straight with your shoulders back, and boldly proclaim, 'I'm a good person!' But the problem is that if you get to invent the criteria for your own goodness, then it's pretty meaningless. In the same way that if I get to draw the bullseye around the arrow *after* I've fired it, then of course I can claim to be an Olympic-level archer. Overall, this is just a recipe for pride and smugness (or for numbing guilt if your tendency is to rate yourself *down* rather than *up*).

What about letting society decide? We could see whether we're *good* or *bad* based on how we measure up to our culture's standards. But then societies can be very, very wrong. Look at historical monstrosities such as slavery (practised by *every* society in the past). Or the Victorians and their disturbing habit of sending children up chimneys and down mines. You can guarantee that our own society has its own moral blind spots which will remain undiagnosed until future generations look back on us and say: 'They did *what*?!?'

So are we at an impasse? Or is there a way forward?

One helpful way we answer the question of whether something is *good* or *bad* is by thinking about its purpose. Consider the humble toaster, for instance. Suppose I try to use my toaster for drying socks and, in so doing, it catches fire. Does that make it a *bad* toaster? Of course not. We determine whether a toaster is a good toaster by how well it toasts bread, bagels, and crumpets; by whether it does what it was designed to do.

So what about human beings—is there anything we were designed to do? Is there any *purpose* to humanity? If Christianity is true, then it tells us we *were* designed for something: to encounter God, to love him, and as we are transformed by that relationship, for it to affect how we relate to others. If Christianity is true, 'good' and 'evil' become words with real meaning—we have God's good purposes and intent for our lives an objective standard against which to measure ourselves.

But, if evolution is the only game in town, we have a problem—one illustrated by Oxford professor C.S. Lewis in his satirical 'Hymn to Evolution':

> Lead us, evolution, lead us,
> Up the future's endless stair,
> Chop us, change us, prod us, weed us,
> For stagnation is despair!
> Groping, guessing, yet progressing,
> Lead us, nobody knows where.[3]

If evolution is *all* that is going on, there's nothing we are *supposed* to be; we are simply one point on the graph of the endless march of evolution. Behind us lies a trail of ancestors all the way back to the primordial soup; ahead of us lies—well, we have no way of knowing. And in such a world, the question of whether we are 'good' and 'bad' becomes meaningless.

The thought that God's purpose for our lives is the plumbline to assess ourselves by, is both philosophically coherent and intellectually satisfying. It can, however, be personally devastating when we realise that in many ways we have fallen short of the ideal. Of course, most of us can point to some things in our lives that seem to fit well with the notion that we have a God-given purpose. But who in all honesty can say they have consistently 'loved their neighbour as they love themselves'?—to cite Jesus's famous command.

In Jesus's view however, God isn't simply the one who sets the standard; he's also the one who forgives and rescues us when we fall short of it. As Nietzsche predicted would happen, our society has lost the art of forgiveness. Thankfully God hasn't.

23

Have you ever wondered if you were created for a purpose?

David Nixon

Have you ever complained about feeling bored or demotivated? As the novelist Mark Twain once remarked: 'The two most important days in your life are the day you are born and the day you find out why.' But is purpose and meaning in life something we can discover, or is it something we have to invent for ourselves? In other words, were you created with a purpose in mind?

Fundamentally, this is a religious and spiritual question, because it forces us to consider what the ultimate nature of reality is. And when it comes to that question, you can divide all the various beliefs, faiths, and worldviews into two broad categories.

First, there is a group of beliefs—perhaps typified by secular humanism or atheist existentialism—that says that everything has *arisen* from nothing and has no ultimate purpose. If you're in this camp, the best you can offer in answer to the meaning question is that purpose is something every human must invent for themselves.

Second, there is another group of beliefs that says that everything was *created* from nothing by *someone* with a purpose. This is the worldview of theism (most notably Judaism and Christianity) and its answer to the meaning question is that meaning is something revealed to us by God our Creator.

Let's compare and contrast these two approaches and see how they might help (or hinder) us as we think about whether our lives have any ultimate kind of point or purpose.

Most of us were taught in school that human beings are the products of nothing more than unguided evolution—we exist because of time, chance, and natural selection. Perhaps we are just blobs of carbon, floating from one meaningless existence to another as some have suggested. That might sound a bit bleak, but for many people it is liberating and appealing; there are no deities to please and no purpose to which you have to conform your life. You are free to, in the words of Frank Sinatra, do life 'my way'!

However, this worldview is not entirely freedom and fun. For example, the atheist philosopher Thomas Nagel admits that taken to its logical conclusion, it's pretty depressing and demotivating:

> *Even if you produce a great work of literature which continues to be read thousands of years from now, eventually the solar system will cool or the universe will wind down and collapse and all trace of your effort will vanish ... It wouldn't matter if you had never existed. And after you have gone out of existence, it won't matter that you did exist.*[1]

If this world and this life is all that there is, then ultimately *nothing* matters. It doesn't matter whether you dedicate yourself to live a life of goodness and generosity or a life of wickedness and selfishness that hurts others—in the end it is all meaningless!

How does that make you feel? Empty ... unfulfilled ... hopeless? Something about this feels wrong—we all need a sense of purpose and meaning to get out of bed in the morning and to hold us back from despairing, or perhaps even suicidal thoughts. Therefore people resort to inventing an individual purpose for themselves. For example, some people live for others, such as their friends or families. Other people choose to live for personal success, perhaps through sporting or academic or workplace performance. Still others dream of doing something that will make an impact on the world through business enterprise or political activism.

Nevertheless, these self-created meanings aren't the full solution. They are too fragile and unfulfilling. Let me introduce you to two people who will explain why.

Firstly, there's Harold Abrahams, the British athlete whose life is chronicled in *Chariots of Fire*. At one point in the film, as he prepares for the next race, Abrahams shares his existential angst:

> *And now in one hour's time I will be out there again ... I will raise my eyes and look down that corridor; four feet wide, with ten lonely seconds to justify my whole existence. But WILL I? ... I'm forever in pursuit and I don't even know what I am chasing.*

Many of us in today's society are a lot like Abrahams—we're running, chasing, pursuing something in this world that will justify and bring value to our existence. However, if your created meaning depends on your performance then you will often be left feeling exhausted, insecure, and anxious as you try to achieve it or try to hold onto it.

Interestingly, the film contrasts Abrahams' mindset with the Scottish Olympic gold medal winning athlete Eric Liddell. Liddell was a Christian and he expresses his perspective on life and running in a conversation with his sister:

> *I believe that God made me for a purpose ... but he also made me fast. And when I run I feel his pleasure.*

His life was given meaning by the fact he knew he was running a greater race with a higher purpose from God—and thus I believe that Liddell points us towards a better answer.

The gospel of John, one of the four historical accounts of the life of Jesus found in the New Testament, begins with these astonishing words:

> *In the beginning was the Word, and the Word was with God and the Word was God. He was with God in the beginning. Through him all things were made ...*[2]

John wrote in Greek and the term translated above as 'the Word' was originally the *Logos*. For centuries before Jesus the greatest Greek thinkers had been searching for the *Logos*: the *Logos* was the logic behind life, the universe, and everything. If you could discover the *Logos*, then it would unlock the secrets of the meaning and purpose of life.

So John wants us to realise that there is an objective meaning and purpose behind the universe. But it is not an impersonal principle to learn in philosophy, but rather a divine person to know in relationship. That's why he goes on to tell us:

> *The Word became flesh and made his dwelling among us. We have seen his glory ...*[3]

John is claiming that the meaning of life is revealed in the person of Jesus Christ, the Son of the Living God! If Jesus is who he claimed to be, we don't need to strive or struggle to construct the 'meaning' of life for ourselves (our efforts doomed to failure), but rather in Jesus, the meaning of life has come to us. God invites us back into a relationship with himself through putting our hope and trust in Jesus—and promises us that within that relationship we will find and fulfil our greatest purpose and potential.

24

Have you ever wondered what God thinks of you?

David Nixon

We hear a lot of discussion these days about the impact of social media and questions are increasingly being raised about the detrimental effect it may be having on our mental health. For example, if you're anything like me, you'll post a status update or picture and then catch yourself repeatedly refreshing your feed to see if people have liked or commented on it. If no one has, then you begin to wonder: 'Does *anyone* care about me?'

Many of us are concerned about what other people think about us, but have you ever wondered, if there's a God, what he thinks of you?

At the heart of the Christian faith lies the astonishing claim that there is nothing that bestows more dignity upon our humanity than the fact that the almighty Creator God became one of us, stepping into history in the person of Jesus. Let me tell you the true story about a man called Nicodemus, who came to meet Jesus 'by night'—which is fitting since Nicodemus is in the dark, unable to see who Jesus is fully, or to see himself truly. You can read his story in chapter 3 of John's gospel, the fourth of the historical biographies of Jesus found in the New Testament.[1]

The first thing we're told about Nicodemus's identity is that he's 'a Pharisee'—that meant Nicodemus was a member of a strict religious order which emphasised rigorous moral behaviour. Secondly, we're told he was 'a member of the Jewish ruling council', which meant he was successful and enjoyed high status. Thirdly, during their conversation Jesus called him 'Israel's teacher', because he was highly educated in the Hebrew Old Testament.

Based on what he knew, what he did, and how other people looked up to him, Nicodemus was a man who might feel very self-satisfied. Perhaps he could be forgiven for imagining that if anyone was in God's good books, qualifying for heaven, then it was him! But just to make sure, Nicodemus comes to see Jesus for a private interview. He'd heard that Jesus performed miracles and spoke as though he were God himself: if that were true, then Nicodemus wondered, what would Jesus make of him? Would Jesus agree with Nicodemus's self-assessment and give him God's stamp of approval?

But Jesus immediately and abruptly challenged Nicodemus by announcing:

'Very truly I tell you, no one can see the kingdom of God unless they are born again.'[2]

That's not something you hear every day so Nicodemus asked the obvious question that we're all thinking:

> *'How can someone be born when they are old?' Nicodemus asked. 'Surely they cannot enter a second time into their mother's womb to be born!'*
>
> *Jesus answered, 'Very truly I tell you, no one can enter the kingdom of God unless they are born of water and the Spirit.'*[3]

Jesus's answer sounds cryptic, but he was drawing on an ancient Old Testament prophecy that one day God was going to do a new thing: transform the rebellious and self-righteous hearts of his people. Jesus explains it's going to take a divine miracle for Nicodemus to be admitted into God's kingdom! Nicodemus is *not* acceptable to God in his current state.

Now this raises a dilemma for us: If the very religious, very good, very knowledgeable, and very respectable Nicodemus doesn't qualify for acceptance into God's kingdom, then what hope do any of us lesser mortals have? The answer is it will take a miracle for us too!

Before you start to think that God is being harsh or unreasonable, it might be helpful to consider the problem facing us in this way:

> *God cannot let me into his kingdom because—as I am—I would spoil it. It is going to be a place of no tears—but I make people cry. It is a place of harmony—but I fall out with people. It's a place of truth—but I lie. And I suspect you do too ... Jesus did not come to help us turn over a new leaf. He came to give us new life—a miracle so radical it would be like a new birth.*[4]

So Jesus confronts each one of us with the bad news that without a miracle, without a radical transformation, we will be excluded from God's new world and perish for ever outside of his good kingdom. That's the *bad* news.

But thankfully there's also some *good* news. This same passage in John's gospel goes on to record some of Jesus's best-known words of comfort and encouragement:

> *For God so loved the world [the world that rejects and ignores him] that he gave his one and only Son, that whoever believes in him shall not perish but have eternal life. For God did not send his Son into the world to condemn the world, but to save the world through him.*[5]

Our rebellion and self-centredness cuts us off and separates us from God—not only is there a gap between our *ideal* self and *actual* self, but there's also a huge gulf between our *actual* self and God—a gap filled with our guilt, shame, regret, and mess-ups. But the good news is that Jesus, God the Son, has come to remove all this rubbish (that the Bible calls 'sin') and restore us into relationship with God his Father.

Jesus wanted Nicodemus to realise, and he wants us today to realise, that acceptance with God and welcome into his new world is not something that we have to strive to achieve, rather it is a free gift that we can receive. Just as we did not contribute anything to bringing ourselves into this world—instead life was a gift from our parents—so also the new birth and new life comes entirely from God and is not based on our own efforts or contributions. Rather it is based entirely on the work Jesus has done for us in his life, death, and resurrection.

So Jesus demonstrates that God sees us truly as we are, behind the masks that we wear; he sees all of the good and all of the bad. And yet despite that, he still chooses to love us and welcome us, mess and all. But he also loves us far too much to leave us in the state in which he finds us. Instead, he wants to help restore us into who he created us to be. God has grand plans and dreams for our lives, both now and for ever!

25

Have you ever wondered if Jesus actually existed?

David Nixon

Our children's library contains many different books recounting the adventures of various characters: *The Gruffalo, Winnie-the-Pooh, Paddington Bear, Thomas the Tank Engine*, and many others. We also have a collection of beautifully illustrated books retelling stories about Jesus from the Bible.

Now, you probably have never lost any sleep over whether or not Winnie-the-Pooh actually existed. Of course we instantly recognise that the honey-loving bear belongs in the realm of fiction. However, have you ever wondered if Jesus really existed? Is *he* fact or fantasy? That's a question that has consumed a significant portion of my life and the lives of many others.

The good news is that it's a question we can answer beyond any reasonable doubt. Even the agnostic New Testament scholar Bart Erhman begins one of his popular books by stating:

I am not a Christian, and I have no interest in promoting a Christian cause or a Christian agenda. I am an agnostic with atheist leanings, and my life and views of the world would be approximately the same whether or not Jesus existed … But as a historian, I think evidence matters. And the past matters. And for anyone to whom both evidence and the past matter, a dispassionate consideration of the case makes it quite plain: Jesus did exist.[1]

We have as much reason to believe that Jesus was a historical figure as we do to believe that Caesar Tiberius existed. There are ten sources documenting Tiberius's existence recorded within 150 years of his life (one of which is a Christian source) whereas for Jesus of Nazareth, we have 42 sources documenting Jesus's existence in the same time-frame (nine of which are non-Christian sources).

In his book *Is Jesus History?*, historian John Dickson takes the reader on a guided tour of those ancient sources that corroborate much of the Bible's testimony about Jesus.[2] For example, there are two mentions of Jesus by the Jewish historian Josephus (*Antiquities* 18:3, 20:9); and one from the Roman historian Tacitus (*Annals* 15:44). Jesus is also discussed by critics who record not only the existence of Jesus but also document that the Christians worshipped Jesus as God from the earliest of times, including:

The Christians, you know, worship a man to this day—the distinguished personage who introduced their novel rites, and was crucified on that account.[3]

Now if the Christians worshipped only one God, they might have reason on their side. But as a matter of fact they worship a man who appeared only recently. They do not consider what they are doing a breach of monotheism; rather they think it perfectly consistent to worship the great God and to worship his servant as God ... When they call him Son of God, they are not really paying homage to God, rather, they are attempting to exalt Jesus to the heights.[4]

So, purely on historical grounds and based on the sources available to historians, it is reasonable to conclude that Jesus really did exist. The more interesting question is why, some two thousand years later, should we *care* that he existed, any more than we care about the Caesars existing?

The philosopher Peter Kreeft reminds us how remarkable it is that we remember Jesus at all:

Jesus never entered politics, never fought a battle, and never wrote a book. He lived in a backwater nation, never went more than one hundred miles of his home and was executed by crucifixion as a dangerous criminal. His moral teachings were not completely new. Nearly every piece of advice he gave us about how to live can be found in his own Jewish tradition, as well as in the philosophies of others. What caused his unparalleled impact?[5]

To answer this question, we need to consult the primary historical sources of those who witnessed the life of Jesus, who watched him perform incredible acts, who heard him claim to be divine. For example, you could take an hour or so one evening to read the shortest and earliest of the gospels—Mark—dated by some scholars to within a decade or two of Jesus's death and resurrection, well within the lifetime of the eyewitnesses.

Throughout his biography of Jesus, Mark's central concern is: *Who is Jesus?* He starts off by announcing the answer, which he seeks to persuade readers of throughout the rest of his book:

> *The beginning of the good news about Jesus the Messiah, the Son of God ...*[6]

In the centre of the book, Mark recounts a conversation between Jesus and his disciples where Jesus asks them: 'And who do you say I am?' Peter, one of the inner circle of twelve disciples, replies with the confession: 'You are the Messiah.'[7] Then almost at the end of his biography, Mark records the proclamation of the Roman centurion who witnessed the death of Jesus: 'Surely this man was the Son of God!'[8] Mark's gospel is all about identifying Jesus.

In the first half of his biography, Mark takes us breathlessly through a series of action-packed stories of Jesus. If you simply skim through these early pages, you'll see:

- Jesus liberates people suffering from evil forces (1:21–28).
- Jesus heals people suffering from diseases (1:29–34).
- Jesus forgives people of their sins and offences against God (2:1–12).
- Jesus calms a storm at sea (4:35–41).
- Jesus heals a woman from an incurable illness and raises a little girl from the dead (5:21–42).

Mark wants us to discover the good news that Jesus can overcome the greatest threats to human flourishing: natural disasters, the power of evil, diseases, and death. He can overcome our failures and wrongdoing too—forgiving us and transforming us. Mark also wants to show us that Jesus not only claims to be God but does things that only God could do!

At the climax of the book, Jesus is arrested and sentenced to death for the crime of blasphemy—of claiming to be the Son of God. Jesus should have been just another forgotten victim of Roman brutality—yet another failed Messiah. However, in the final chapter of Mark's gospel we read the account of the first eyewitnesses to the empty tomb. Jesus had risen from the dead—vindicating his startling claims to be the Son of God and the Lord of life.

Strangely, however, Mark ends his biography on a minor key:

> *Trembling and bewildered, the women went out and fled from the tomb. They said nothing to anyone, because they were afraid.*[9]

Obviously, that wasn't the end of the story—much more happened afterwards. But the question is why does Mark end his biography this way? It seems Mark is wanting to draw you, the reader, into the story. He's challenging you—now that you know who Jesus is, it's your job to respond to the story. Who do *you* say that Jesus is?

26

Have you ever wondered if all religions are basically the same?

Andy Bannister

I grew up in a very diverse part of London. Where I lived as a teenager, you could choose from many different belief systems: Buddhism, Hinduism, Sikhism, and many other *isms*. Religion was *everywhere* and today, a few decades on, it's still everywhere—and growing. According to the statistics, people don't believe *less*, but they do believe far more diversely.[1]

One reason for this growth is that people are increasingly dissatisfied with shallow secular answers, such as the idea that all you need is money and pleasure, and that's enough. As psychiatrist and author Viktor Frankl famously put it: 'Ever more people today have the means to live, but no meaning to live for.'

How do we answer that *meaning* question? Winifred Gallagher is a journalist who has written for magazines including *Rolling*

Stone and *The Atlantic*. In an interview about her book, *Working on God*, Winifred described a growing unease in our culture, the sense that there must be more to life:

> *The only way to describe the new phenomenon I am observing is to coin a new phrase: spiritual agnostics. We have regarded religion as belief in unbelievable things. Our trusted tools of intellect and learning have deconstructed religious belief. But we're finding that we have inexplicable feelings. We wonder: Is this true? Is this all there is? I have tried to muffle this question in all the accustomed ways all my life: love, achievement, stuff, and therapy. I tried to muffle it by writing two books on science. By middle age, I have wearily recognized that religion is the only road I have not taken in pursuit of the answer … We're haunted by faith.*[2]

If, as Winifred discovered, we are spiritual beings who need more than the endless treadmill of career to satisfy us, that raises a deeper question: *which* religion? Many people, when they realise there's a spiritual side to life, quickly panic when they see the incredible range of religious options available. Paralysed by choice, it's tempting to reach for easy platitudes, such as: 'Most probably *all* religions teach basically the same thing.' That's a warm, comfortable idea, not least because it allows us to approach spirituality in a slightly consumerist way, picking the beliefs, ideas, or practices that 'work for us': a little bit of yoga, a dash of meditation, the odd prayer, a couple of candles, and a lemon-scented journal.

But the uncomfortable fact remains that the only way to maintain the belief that all religions are more or less the same is by not actually going and looking at them. For you don't have to look for long before you stumble across major differences between the world's major faiths and spiritual traditions. To give one significant example, consider Christianity and Islam: examining the character of God in the Bible, you discover that God is relational, knowable and is not just loving, but *is* love. Turn to the Qur'an, and you discover its claims about God are almost entirely the opposite.[3]

'Ah, but that's just theology,' you say. However, turning to history, we find sizable differences too. The central event of the Christian faith is the death and resurrection of Jesus; secular historians will tell you that the former is one of the best attested facts of first-century history. The evidence that Jesus was crucified, under the Roman governor Pilate, sometime round about AD 33, is overwhelming. But the Qur'an, written some 600 years later, claims that Jesus was not killed by crucifixion, and this was just a wild claim made by the Jews. Those two historical claims—*crucified* and *not-crucified*—are impossible to reconcile.

And the more you study Christianity and Islam, indeed the more you compare any of the world's faith traditions, the more the contradictions mount up. So how do we navigate the maze of diversity and difference?

To begin with, don't be worried by it. It's just one more sign that human beings are inherently religious, that we're wired for spirituality. The fact that a desire for connection with God bubbles up universally in humanity, across time and culture, is itself a massive clue. But that aside, how do we work through all the options and choices? Do we just pick randomly and hope for the best—or is there a better way?

I think there is. And my first suggestion is: try praying. If there is a God behind this universe and religious truth to be discovered, why not ask for help? After all, Jesus famously said: 'Ask and it will be given to you; seek and you will find; knock and the door will be opened to you.'[4] You could perhaps pray something like: *'God, I don't know what to believe about you, but I want to know the truth and I want to encounter you. Please guide my steps as I seek.'*

Secondly, try reading the stories of those who have trodden the path of spiritual inquiry before you, especially those who have had the courage to follow that path out of the religious tradition where they began. One of the most inspiring books I have ever read is Nabeel Qureshi's autobiography, *Seeking Allah, Finding Jesus.* It tells the story of how, as a young and highly devout Muslim, Nabeel set out on a quest to know God better—and that journey led him not deeper into Islam, but to a life-changing encounter with Jesus.

Thirdly, take a careful look at Jesus—perhaps by reading one of the four first-century eyewitness biographies about him found in the New Testament. Many religions claim to offer wisdom, advice, or high-minded thoughts about God—but Christianity teaches that God stepped into history in Jesus, in order to *show* us what he is like. And Jesus shows us a God offering connection, forgiveness, and transformation.

But one final thought. It's been remarked by many anthropologists that you can divide the world's religions into three groups: based on whether they think what is most important is *thinking,* or *feeling,* or *doing.*

In religions based on *thinking,* you have to memorise and master the right ideas in order to achieve salvation, wisdom, or a higher state of existence. In religions based on *feeling,* it's by pursuing the right experience that you try to make some kind of connection with the divine. Whilst in religions based on *doing*, it's by working hard to obey the religion's commands and laws that you aim to get closer to paradise, heaven, or god.

But in each case, notice where the effort lies. It's *your* thinking, *your* feelings, or *your* actions that are what drag you up the ladder to the divine. I don't know about you, but the pressure of that terrifies me. How can you be sure you've learnt enough, experienced enough, or done enough? You can never be secure—and should you think you *have* made it, well that's no better, because that just leads to arrogance as you look down on others from the tower of your lofty self-righteousness.

There is only one religion I know that breaks this pattern—and that's what Jesus taught. Jesus didn't say he'd come to bring new information to learn, or new experiences to chase after, or new commands to keep. Rather he claimed to be God *with us*, God come to search for us, to close the gap between us and heaven by his efforts, not by ours.

Do all religions lead to God? It's a profound question. But have you ever wondered if *no* religion leads to God, maybe only God can lead us to God. Which is, fascinatingly, precisely what Jesus believed his life, death, and resurrection was all about.

27

___

Have you ever wondered where everything is going?

Gavin Matthews

We tend to associate the term 'market research' with annoying people intercepting us in the street to ask us which brand of washing powder we prefer the taste of. But a group of researchers recently set out to study something far more meaningful: What are the big questions of life that people across the country are asking and which are the most pressing?

The results provided a fascinating snapshot of our culture at this point in time.[1] The question that topped the list (beating 'What happens when you die?' into second place) was, 'Will everything be OK?' This is probably not surprising given that the survey took place against the backdrop of the three Ps: pandemics, poverty, and Putin; stark reminders of the perennial fragility of life.

In 1990, when former Cold-War adversaries Russia and NATO worked with the UN to restore the independence of

127

Kuwait after it was invaded, a 'New World Order' was heralded. International cooperation for peace and prosperity, replacing the half-century threat of nuclear annihilation and incessant proxy-wars around the globe, was to be the 'new normal'. Our political leaders, we were assured, hadn't just secured peace and prosperity, but tyranny and dictatorship were in retreat around the globe—and democratic freedom was on the march from South Africa to St Petersburg. We were privileged to live on the cusp of a bright future.

But as we know, the uprisings which felled dictatorships across Eastern Europe were not replicated in China. The so-called Arab Spring was far from being the harbinger of liberality that many at the time claimed it to be. In 2008, the 'credit crunch' caused a worldwide economic recession. There were the 9/11 attacks, controversial Western military interventions in Iraq and Afghanistan, and the rise of the Taliban and ISIS. Then the world was hit by the COVID-19 pandemic. Lockdowns were imposed, and as the dust settled, there followed an economic crash unprecedented in peacetime, and use of the word unprecedented reached hitherto *unprecedented* levels. By 2022, the world was just limping back in search of the promised New World Order when Vladimir Putin launched his invasion of Ukraine. Twenty years ago, Europe had claimed to have healed its divisions and could export its brand of peace to the world. But Europe was at war again. And peace certainly hadn't been brought to the world as numerous conflicts have painfully demonstrated, not least the Israel-Hamas war which broke out in 2023.

No wonder 'Will everything be OK?' tops the questions people are asking today. We are the generation sold the false prospectus that the problems we face are within our capacity to fix, and that the right people were on the case. However, our optimism was ill-founded.

In 2018 a new word, *doomscrolling*, was coined. It means the insatiable desire to gaze at your phone, reading news story after news story, all the while feeling bleaker and bleaker. With the average person spending nearly two and a half hours a day on social media,[2] doomscrolling has become for many of us an *addiction*, and countless internet pages are devoted to counselling us as how to escape from its clutches. Everyone seems to be wondering where it is all going.

Is anyone in control? Is the story of this world one with a storyteller, in which the narrative reaches some kind of closure? Or is blind chance and pure luck the only explanation for every delight, drudgery, or disaster which weaves its way in and out of our lives? Will the random forces of time and chance defeat us all in the end? As planet earth hurtles through space at 67,000 mph, we all want to know whether there's a hand on the tiller.

Many find the thought that there *isn't* anyone in control quite alarming.

When Turkey and Syria were rocked by an horrific earthquake in early 2023, the BBC news interviewed a Turkish man standing on what had once been a block of flats, deep in grief for those whose bodies lay beneath the rubble. His view was that the tragedy was not the result of impersonal geological forces, but rather it had been willed specifically by his God, Allah. 'This is a test,' he explained.

Many find the thought that there's a God in control of everything who specifically willed all of this *also* quite alarming.

Are we really forced to choose between nihilism or a deity who looks at the very least unsympathetic to our weaknesses?

What kind of choice is that?

Others look for some middle ground between these two extremes. The Hindu guru Sri Sri Ravi Shankar argues that while events on earth are not random, equally they are not imposed upon us by a deity, rather they are the outworking of impersonal spiritual laws. The dualistic law of karma means that:

> … you have to pay some debt, and so you are undergoing what you are undergoing. But do not think that every problem or suffering that you go through is only because of your actions from past lifetimes. Some of it also comes because of the foolishness and ignorance from the present lifetime also.[3]

Many find the thought that suffering is some form of spiritual re-balancing and that there might be no means of escape from it through endless life cycles … quite alarming.

Is there any other way of approaching this conundrum?

Wouldn't it be wonderful if there might be some sort of God who is ultimately taking history in a definite direction, but who doesn't spend his days singling people out for cancer, earthquakes, or lightning bolts? Is it just possible there might be a God who gives humans real responsibility and genuine agency, but who also offers a gracious exit from the fear of endless cycles of karma? Have you ever wondered if there is a God who rather than standing apart from this world's sin and pain has entered it and tasted it, in order to rescue it? A God who might be nearby and not far away?[4]

If you have ever wondered this, then I gently suggest that you have actually been wondering about Jesus of Nazareth.

Because if Jesus is who he claimed to be—God stepping into space, time, and history—then his promise to return one day to bring about the genuine and good 'end of history' can be trusted too. Things could get worse before they get better, but if Jesus is right, the world is not ultimately spinning out of control but awaiting its rescuer.

Have you ever wondered if you can truly change?

Gareth Black

All of us love stories about transformation. Whether it's an inspirational account of someone's weight-loss journey or the Cinderella story of an athlete who against all odds reaches the pinnacle of their sport, our attraction to tales of metamorphosis runs deep. And so often it's the stories about changes in people's characters that are most *deeply* intriguing to us: who a person is, or becomes, at the deepest level of their nature and personality.

Consider how widespread this idea of character transformation is within storytelling. Sometimes that change is a tragic one, as we follow a protagonist degenerating hopelessly into psychological and moral catastrophe—think of Shakespeare's Macbeth, or *Game of Thrones'* Daenerys Targaryen.

But our most beloved stories are often those that portray radical transformation in the *opposite* direction. These are the tales of redemption, where a formerly corrupt and detestable character emerges transfigured, born again as a now morally virtuous, admirable individual: think of Jean Valjean in *Les Misérables,* or the Grinch, who stole Christmas but had a change of heart and gave it back again!

Have you ever wondered why the idea of transformation resonates so meaningfully with us? Might the reason why these stories connect with us so profoundly be because of their plausibility—that as we observe them, we are in some sense looking into the mirror of our own faculty for change in either moral direction?

The Russian writer Aleksandr Solzhenitsyn once observed that 'the line dividing good and evil cuts through the heart of every human being'.[1] As we read stories of transformation, they read *us*; they imaginatively remind us of our primal capacity for both evil or good, a *fall from grace* or glorious *redemption*.

But beyond our mere love for the *idea* of transformation, how achievable is change in the real world? Is transformation just a romantic pipe dream or a realistic hope?

When it comes to physical alteration at least, it would appear that the promise of change is incredibly believable. The multi-billion-dollar success of the fitness, weight-loss, and cosmetics industries are testament to the marketability of the promise of transformation.

But what about *character* change?

I wonder if real change appears unattainable to many of us because of disappointing personal experience. Perhaps we once put our faith in an assurance from a spouse, a parent or a child that from now on, things would be different—only to painfully discover nothing changed. Leopards cannot change their spots.

Or perhaps the frustration is in some area of our own lives and we have wearily resigned ourselves to the fact that things will always be the same.

In a thought-provoking article entitled, 'Why Most People Don't Really Change', author and psychotherapist Joseph Burgo offers three reasons why people often fail to change.[2] We find character transformation so difficult, Burgo says, because: a) most people don't have an accurate view of who they truly are and, therefore, don't recognise where they might need to change; b) we have a human propensity to blame other people for our shortcomings (e.g. family or political systems); and c) effecting change involves hard work and making difficult choices.

If Burgo's diagnoses are correct, it would seem that our only hope of true change is to find a meaningful source of *light, love, and power*. We need a *light* that can accurately and indiscriminately illuminate the reality of who and what we are; we need a *love* that will patiently continue to believe in us and pursue our ultimate good, despite the ugliness of what the light may reveal; and we need a *power* that can authentically change us at the deepest levels of our humanity.

What is so interesting is that in many of the tales of transformation we enjoy, this *light, love, and power* is discovered not by an individual's introspection nor by personal willpower, but via an external—often supernatural—agent that intervenes over the course of a character's life. This was certainly the case for old Ebenezer Scrooge. It was the painful, yet loving supernatural light of what three ghosts revealed that awakened Scrooge to his true condition and empowered his transformation from a man who lived in darkness and misery to becoming 'as good a friend, as good a master, and as good a man as the good old city knew'.

I wonder if that is why many people also find Christianity so compelling. After all, Jesus claimed not simply to provide light, but to be *the* Light of the World.[3] He promised that whoever followed him would never walk in darkness but would have light that empowers life as it is meant to be lived. At the heart of the Christian faith lies not an exhortation to try harder to do better, but rather the promise that when we put our faith in Jesus, then God's power makes us 'new creations'—new at the very deepest level of our nature—so that we then begin to think, act, and feel from this place of transformation.

This promise and power of Jesus to truly change us is a claim that is testable, for it is a promise that has been personally verified by millions of people down through history. For example, ask my friend Thomas A. Tarrants, a former violent Ku Klux Klansman once consumed by hate, but who upon following Jesus was transformed and became a champion of racial reconciliation and one of the most loving men I have ever met.[4] Or think of John Newton, the eighteenth-century slave trader who was radically converted to Christianity and became a clergyman and abolitionist, penning perhaps the most famous song about character change ever written:

> *Amazing grace, how sweet the sound,*
> *That saved a wretch like me;*
> *I once was lost, but now am found,*
> *Was blind but now I see.*

Now there's a story of transformation. And it's not fiction, but biography.

So if you've ever wondered if real change is possible—if it's possible even for you—can I encourage you to keep looking into Christianity. For as the atheist journalist Matthew Parris once confessed in *The Times* newspaper: 'Christianity changes people's hearts. It brings a spiritual transformation. The rebirth is real. The change is good.'[5]

Conclusion

———

Have you ever wondered where to look for answers?

Andy Bannister

There is a scene in *The Lord of the Rings* where the wizard Gandalf is guiding the Fellowship through the darkness of the ruined dwarf mines of Moria. They come to a point where the tunnel divides into three and Gandalf remarks, 'I have no memory of this place' and they come to a halt. After a few hours of thought, during which his companions worry that they are lost for ever in the dark, Gandalf finally pipes up: 'Ah! It's that way', pointing down the right-hand tunnel. 'He's remembered!' cries the hobbit, Merry. 'No,' replies Gandalf, 'but the air doesn't smell so foul down there. If in doubt, Meriadoc, always follow your nose!'[1]

Within the pages of this book we have explored some twenty-eight different but universal human experiences and in each case we've wondered together about what they mean, why they matter to us, and how we make sense of them. And in each case we've also encountered a choice of paths. One fork in the road offers a purely material universe, but as we've seen time and again, followed all the way, this leads us further into the darkness. If reducing the universe to the laws of physics and humanity to just the atoms and molecules of which we're made means kissing goodbye to meaning, love, purpose, music, justice, and everything else—then the sheer foulness of that conclusion means we should give the other routes a serious look.

The second fork in the road explored in chapter 26 is the path of religion and spirituality, acknowledging there is some sort of higher power and seeking to prove ourselves worthy. But when we're honest with ourselves, we, like the Fellowship, need outside help to make it through. We all have a mix of good and bad within us, and we're unable to truly change on our own (as we saw in chapter 28). Striving to be good enough is a disheartening dead end.

The third fork is the way of Jesus. And just like Gandalf in Moria, I want to suggest that one very good reason for considering Jesus carefully is because the air does smell fresher that way. Living in a created universe, and made in the image of God, our instincts about the value of our lives, of sex, of the past, of beauty, of all the things we hold as precious, prove true. We can be real with ourselves and come to Jesus for the forgiveness and restoration that each one of us needs.

Jesus's offer is unique—his death paid for all our debts, and instead of being alienated from God, we can be welcomed in when we turn to him, without having to earn the privilege. We can find ourselves, and our future, in Jesus. We don't need to fear death because Jesus conquered it by rising again and he will one day put all things right. You may not feel at all ready to follow this third path at the moment, but if so much that we hold dear turns to dust and ashes if Christianity isn't true, then surely it's at least worth a look.

But I realise that for many of us even that first step can be a difficult one. If you've been told since you were a child that matter is all that exists and that only fools believe in God. If you've been turned off 'religion' by some of the nastiness that has all too often marched under that flag. If you've had a bad experience of church or Christians in the past and still bear the wounds. If you're afraid of your friends sniggering when you admit that you're wondering if there might be something to this whole God business. I have no doubt that being a comfortable agnostic, sitting on the fence, can sometimes look more tempting than the journey of spiritual exploration.

Yet so much stands or falls on whether Jesus is who he claimed to be. All of the topics we've looked at in this book really matter; they're what make life worth living. And if none of them make sense if there is no God, then faith surely must at least be worth the look. If you're stranded in a desert and dying of thirst, not every glimmer on the horizon is water—after all, there's a risk it's a mirage—but with so much at stake, surely it's worth the walk to see?

In his book *Life After God*, which explores the attempts of his generation to try to do away with God and invent their own meaning to life, Canadian novelist Douglas Coupland concludes with this paragraph:

> *Now here is my secret: I tell it to you with an openness of*
> *heart that I doubt I shall ever achieve again, so I pray you are*
> *in a quiet room as you hear these words. My secret is that I*
> *need God—that I am sick and can no longer make it alone. I*
> *need God to help me give, because I no longer seem capable of*
> *giving; to help me to be kind, as I no longer seem capable of*
> *kindness; to help me love, as I seem beyond being able to love.[2]*

My guess is that if you've picked up *Have You Ever Wondered?* and have read this far, you may be nodding in agreement at Coupland's words. Yet it's one thing to admit that so many things only make sense if God is real, but it's another to know what to do with this thought. What's the next step? Let me suggest some steps for the spiritual journey that you might consider.

First, try praying. Even if you've never prayed before, you might try what is sometimes known as the seeker's prayer: *God, I don't know what I believe about you. I don't even know if I believe you exist. But I want to know. And I believe if you're real, you'd want me to know. God, if you're there, please would you guide my journey as I think more about you.*

Second, if you were given this book by a friend, why not ask them for their thoughts and advice, or to tell you their story of faith. Ask your friend what their experience of God has been, why they believe what they believe. And given they're *probably* a Christian, ask what they think about Jesus—and why.

Third, take a look at Jesus. If all the things we've looked at in this book are signposts, many times we've found they're not so much pointing at a *what* but a *who*. And the exciting news of Christianity is that if you want to know what God is really like, take a look at Jesus. So pick up a Bible and read the gospel of Mark, the shortest (and earliest) of the four first-century biographies of Jesus's life. You could also grab a copy of *A Doubter's Guide to Jesus*, by the historian John Dickson. It's a brilliant introduction to Jesus's life and impact.

Fourth, if your reaction to Jesus and Christianity is 'But what about … X?' where X is a question, issue, or objection, then check out the *Short Answers* video series on the Solas website at solas-cpc.org/shortanswers—it's got loads of five-minute answers to hundreds of questions.

Fifth, do more reading. There are a number of great books out there which continue to explore the big questions—why the world, and everyone in it, is so broken; why Jesus came to die and rise again; and how he can reconnect us to God. *Who Is Jesus?* by Roger Carswell, *How to See Life: A Guide in 321* by Glen Scrivener or *The Truth About Lies* by J. Mack Stiles would all be good places to start.

Sixth, try a course along with others exploring the Christian faith. Lots of churches around the world run the Alpha and Christianity Explored courses. These combine a chance to learn more about Jesus with the space to ask any question you like— and often in the context of food and friendship. Find a course near you at alpha.org.uk/try or christianityexplored.org.

Seventh and finally, why not try a local church? Many churches are full of people of all ages, from those who are long-time followers of Jesus to those who are there to check out Christianity, walking around it kicking the tyres a bit. We realise that can be a daunting step if you've never been to one, so feel free to email us direct at hyew@solas-cpc.org, letting us know your town or city, and we'll try and put you in touch with a church.

I've suggested that the twenty-eight topics we've thought about are signposts. And the thing about a signpost is you aren't supposed to just look *at* it. ('What a lovely signpost! Look at the way the light strikes it, the beautiful font they've used …!') Rather, of course, you're supposed to look where it's pointing. I hope over these many chapters we've been able to persuade you that all these signposts point to Jesus. Individually, each example might be contrived or a coincidence, but taken together, they're compelling. Have you ever wondered if it's time to finally explore where they're pointing?

Endnotes

Chapter 1

1   I owe this insight to my Canadian friend John Patrick. His 'Four Levels of Happiness' approach is based in turn on Robert Spitzer, *Ten Universal Principles: A Brief Philosophy of the Life Issues* (Ignatius Press, 2011), pp. 91–101.

2   Matthew 11:28.

3   John 10:10.

Chapter 2

1   Most love stories contain obstacles—or people—to overcome (think Mr Wickham in *Pride and Prejudice*). And even in dystopian fiction, like Orwell's *Nineteen Eighty-Four*, as a reader you're meant to protest; not cheer at the triumph of Big Brother.

2   Humphrey Carpenter, ed., *The Letters of J.R.R. Tolkien* (Houghton Mifflin, 2000), p. 172.

3   See Jonathan Petre, 'Christianity Inspired Harry Potter', *The Telegraph* (20 October 2007). Available at: https://www.telegraph.co.uk/culture/books/fictionreviews/3668658/J-K-Rowling-Christianity-inspired-Harry-Potter.html.

4   A lovely phrase coined by Tolkien.

Chapter 3

1   Josie Griffiths, 'Dismal Disney', *The Sun* (23 Oct 2017). Available at: https://www.thesun.co.uk/fabulous/4746372/gruesome-original-ending-hunchback-notre-dame/.

2   Bertrand Russell, 'A Free Man's Worship' (1903), available online at: https://www3.nd.edu/~afreddos/courses/264/fmw.htm.

3   To quote Richard Dawkins's infamous phrase in *River out of Eden* (Basic Book, 1995), pp. 131–132.

4   For more on this, see Tom Holland, *Dominion* (Little, Brown, 2019); Vishal Mangalwadi, *The Book That Made Your World* (Thomas Nelson,

2011); Alister McGrath, *In The Beginning: The Story of the King James Bible and How It Changed a Nation, a Language and a Culture* (Anchor Books 2021); Glen Scrivener, *The Air We Breathe: How We All Came to Believe in Freedom, Kindness, Progress, and Equality* (The Good Book Company, 2022); Nick Spencer, *The Evolution of the West* (SPCK, 2016).

Chapter 4

1   Michael Shermer, 'Why People Believe Invisible Agents Control the World', *Scientific American* (1 June 2009). Available at: https://www.scientificamerican.com/article/skeptic-agenticity/.

2   Cited in Tiffanie Wen, 'Why Do People Believe in Ghosts?', *The Atlantic* (5 September 2014). Available at: https://www.theatlantic.com/health/archive/2014/09/why-do-people-believe-in-ghosts/379072/.

3   Aldous Huxley, 'Confessions of a Professed Atheist', *Report: Perspective on the News*, Vol. 3 (June 1996), p. 19.

Chapter 5

1   Aristotle, *Nicomachean Ethics*, book 1, trans. Sarah Broadie and Christopher Rowe (Open University Press, 2002), p. 95.

2   Matthew 6:25, 33–34 (emphasis added).

Chapter 6

1   Psalm 27:4.

2   One could argue that Cage's piece is an interpretation of the beauty of the everyday incidental sounds of humans. But, in my music education background, I noticed how many trained musicians have an abject dislike of this piece of 'music', which seems to deconstruct the meaning of the term beyond any reconciliation. In other words, it *really* annoys us.

3   Fiona MacDonald, 'Here's How Colours Really Affect Our Brain and Body, According to Science', *ScienceAlert* (28 September 2017). Available at: https://www.sciencealert.com/does-colour-really-affect-our-brain-and-body-a-professor-of-colour-science-explains.

4   Louise Lankston et al., 'Visual Art in Hospitals: Case Studies and Review of the Evidence', *Journal of the Royal Society of Medicine* (1 December 2010). Available at: https://journals.sagepub.com/doi/10.1258/jrsm.2010.100256.

5   Kristophe Green and Dacher Keltner 'What Happens When We Reconnect with Nature', *Greater Good Magazine* (1 March 2017). Available at: https://greatergood.berkeley.edu/article/item/what_happens_when_we_reconnect_with_nature.

Chapter 7

1 'William McFadzean VC', *Royal Irish* (no date). Available at: https://www.royal-irish.com/persons/william-mcfadzean-vc.

2 Richard Dawkins, 'Preface to the First Edition', *The Selfish Gene* (Oxford University Press, 2006), p. xxi.

3 Charles Dickens, *A Tale of Two Cities* (Signet Classics, 2007), p. 365.

4 1 John 3:16.

Chapter 8

1 Alex Rosenberg, *The Atheist's Guide to Reality: Enjoying Life Without Illusions* (W.W. Norton Company, 2011), p. 162.

2 Ibid., 2–3.

Chapter 9

1 Bertrand Russell, 'The Study of Mathematics', *The New Quarterly* 1 (November 1907). Available at: https://users.drew.edu/~jlenz/br-ml-ch4.html.

2 The symbol for the imaginary number defined as i2 = -1. I remember, when the concept of imaginary numbers was first introduced to me as a teenager, I complained to my teacher: 'Real numbers are awful enough, why would anybody want to make up more of the things?'

3 Jim Al-Khalili made this comment during an appearance on the *Premier Unbelievable* podcast episode 'Who invented the universe?' Available at https://podcasts.apple.com/gb/podcast/unbelievable/id267142101?i=1000354571909.

4 Eugene Wigner, 'The Unreasonable Effectiveness of Mathematics in the Natural Sciences', *Communications in Pure and Applied Mathematics,* Vol. 13, No. 1 (February 1960). Available at: https://www.maths.ed.ac.uk/~v1ranick/papers/wigner.pdf.

5 Ibid. (emphasis added).

6 Douglas Adams, *The Hitchhiker's Guide to the Galaxy* (Harmony Books, 1979), pp. 179–181.

Chapter 10

1 Patricia S. Churchland, 'Epistemology in the Age of Neuroscience', *Journal of Philosophy*, Vol. 84, No. 10 (1987), p. 584. Quoted in Timothy Keller, *The Reason for God* (Hodder & Stoughton, 2009), p. 137.

2 *Broken Planet* by Sharon Dirckx and *Where is God in all the Suffering?* by Amy Orr Ewing would be good starting places. See also chapter 19, 'Have you ever wondered why suffering and evil seem so wrong?'

3   From C.S. Lewis's sermon, 'The Weight of Glory', first preached in the University Church of St Mary the Virgin, Oxford, on 8 June 1941. It was published in *Theology*, Vol. 43 (November 1941), pp. 263–74, and later in 1949 by Macmillan in New York as *The Weight of Glory, and Other Addresses*.

4   Paul Gould, *Cultural Apologetics* (Zondervan, 2019), p. 117.

Chapter 11

1   Genesis 1:27.

2   Isaiah 55:8–9.

3   Cited in Amanda Lohrey, 'The Big Nothing: Lawrence Krauss and Arse-Kicking Physics', *The Monthly* (October 2012). Available at: https://www.themonthly.com.au/issue/2012/october/1354074365/amanda-lohrey/big-nothing#mtr.

Chapter 12

1   Smitha Mundasad, 'Black Women Four Times More Likely to Die in Childbirth', BBC (11 November 2021). Available at: https://www.bbc.co.uk/news/health-59248345.

2   Sally Weale and Vikram Dodd, 'Revealed: Met Police Strip-Search 650 Children in Two-Year Period', *The Guardian* (8 August 2022). Available at: https://www.theguardian.com/uk-news/2022/aug/08/police-data-raises-alarm-over-welfare-of-strip-searched-children.

3   'Permanent Exclusions', Gov UK (7 February 2023). Available at: https://www.ethnicity-facts-figures.service.gov.uk/education-skills-and-training/absence-and-exclusions/permanent-exclusions/latest.

4   'Rate of use of force (in relation to white ethnic group) by the police in England and Wales in 2022/23, by ethnicity', Statista Research Department (5 January 2024). Available at: https://www.statista.com/statistics/1230747/police-use-of-force-rate-england-and-wales-by-ethnicity/#:~:text=In%20the%202022%2F23%20reporting,against%20them%20by%20police%20forces.

5   Sean Coughlan, 'Poorer White Pupils Let Down and Neglected—MPs', BBC (22 June 2021). Available at: https://www.bbc.co.uk/news/education-57558746.

6   For more information about Masterclass see: https://masterclassedu.co.uk/.

7   Frederick Douglass, *Narrative of the Life of Frederick Douglass* (1845), Kindle edition, chapter XIX.

8   Genesis 1:27.

9   Ephesians 2:10.

10   John 3:16.

Chapter 13

1   Fay Bound Alberti, *A Biography of Loneliness: The History of an Emotion* (Oxford University Press, 2019).

Chapter 14

1   Louise Perry, *The Case Against the Sexual Revolution: A New Guide to Sex in the 21st Century* (Polity Press, 2022), p. 150.

2   Ecclesiastes 1:9.

3   'Sexual Attitudes and Lifestyle in Britain: Highlights from Natsal-3', *Natsal* (2013). Available at: https://www.natsal.ac.uk/sites/default/files/2021-04/Natsal-3%20infographics%20%281%29_0.pdf. See also Louise Perry, *The Case Against the Sexual Revolution: A New Guide to Sex in the 21st Century* (Polity Press, 2022) for a discussion of the changes in attitudes towards sex.

4   Olivia Petter, 'Nearly Half of British Women Dissatisfied with Sex Lives, Survey Finds', *The Independent* (26 June 2018). Available at https://www.independent.co.uk/life-style/health-and-families/women-sex-lives-how-good-satisfied-british-public-health-england-a8417126.html.

5   Jim Mann, 'British Sex Survey: "The Nation has Lost Some of its Sexual Swagger"', *The Guardian* (28 Sept 2014). Available at: https://www.theguardian.com/lifeandstyle/2014/sep/28/british-sex-survey-2014-nation-lost-sexual-swagger.

6   The average is now 6–10 with the mean being 9.5. Ibid.

7   Quoted in Olga Khazan, 'Fewer Sex Partners Means a Happier Marriage', *The Atlantic* (22 October 2018). Available at: https://www.theatlantic.com/health/archive/2018/10/sexual-partners-and-marital-happiness/573493/

8   Isaiah 62:5.

Chapter 15

1   Margaret Atwood, *The Handmaid's Tale* (Vintage, 1996), p. 237.

2   John 15:13.

3   'The Heroic Role of the Titanic's Engineers', *The Guardian* (10 April 2012). Available at: https://www.theguardian.com/uk/2012/apr/10/heroic-role-titanic-engineer.

4   Romans 5:8 (emphasis added).

Chapter 16

1   Peter Singer, 'Sanctity of Life or Quality of Life', *Pediatrics*, Vol. 72, Issue 1 (1983), pp. 128–129.

2   Ekemini Uwan, *Truth's Table: Black Women's Musings on Life, Love and Liberation* (Convergent, 2022), p.273.

Chapter 17

1   Rebecca Atkinson, 'National Trust Sees Membership Rise Following Pandemic', *Museums Association* (9 September 2022). Available at: www.museumsassociation.org/museums-journal/news/2022/09/national-trust-sees-membership-rise-following-pandemic. See also: https://www.independent.co.uk/news/uk/english-heritage-tintagel-castle-yorkshire-cornwall-london-b2279470.html.

2   'Our Work', *National Trust for Scotland*. Available at: https://www.nts.org.uk/our-work.; 'Our Annual Report 2021–22', *Historic Environment Scotland* (22 Nov 2022). Available at: https://www.historicenvironment.scot/about-us/news/our-annual-report-2021-22/#:~:text=we%20continued%20to%20feel%20the,and%20management%20of%20the%20PiCs.

3   'Facts and figures of the British Library', *British Library*. Available at: https://www.bl.uk/about-us/our-story/facts-and-figures-of-the-british-library.

4   Tim Harford's *Cautionary Tales* podcast is available at https://timharford.com/articles/cautionarytales/.

5   That means it's available in languages spoken by 80% of the world's population. Simon Bartz, 'Full Bible Translation Tops 700 Languages for First Time', *The Bible Society* (7 August 2020). Available at: https://www.biblesociety.org.uk/latest/news/full-bible-translation-tops-700-languages-for-first-time/.

6   See chapter 3 in Elijah Hixson and Peter J. Gurry, *Myths and Mistakes in New Testament Textual Criticism* (IVP Academic, 2019).

7   See for example Vishal Mangalwadi, *The Book That Made Your World: How the Bible Created the Soul of Western Civilization* (Thomas Nelson, 2011).

8   Luke 22:19.

Chapter 18

1   Psalm 139:14.

Chapter 19

1   Richard Dawkins, *River out of Eden* (1995), pp. 131–132.

2   C.S. Lewis, *Mere Christianity* (Harper Collins, 2001 [1952]), pp. 38–39.

3   Timothy Keller, *The Reason for God: Belief in an Age of Skepticism* (Dutton, 2008), p. 30.

4   For an overview of the historical evidence for the resurrection, see Michael R. Licona, 'A Beginner's Guide to the Evidence for the Resurrection', *Solas* (13 April 2020). Available at: https://www.solas-cpc.org/a-beginners-guide-to-the-evidence-for-the-resurrection/.

Chapter 20

1   Amy Orr-Ewing, *Where is God in all the Suffering?* (The Good Book Company, 2020), pp. 22–23.

2   Isaiah 59:9–10.

Chapter 21

1   Quoted in The Daily Dish, 'What Do Atheists Think of Death?' *The Atlantic* (16 May 2010). Available at: https://www.theatlantic.com/daily-dish/archive/2010/05/what-do-atheists-think-of-death/187003/.

2   Leo Nikolayevich Tolstoy, *A Confession* (Christian Classics Ethereal Library, 1998 [1882]) p. 16.

3   YouGov Death Study conducted 19–23 March 2021 on a sample of 2,164 UK adults aged 16 and older. Milan Dinic, 'YouGov Death Study', YouGov UK (6 October 2021). Available at: https://yougov.co.uk/topics/lifestyle/articles-reports/2021/10/06/yougov-death-study-britons-their-funeral-and-how-l.

4   Harry Atkins, 'Did Shakespeare Really Write His Own Plays?', *History Hit* (10 April 2022). Available at: https://www.historyhit.com/culture/did-shakespeare-really-write-his-own-plays/.

5   Ecclesiastes 1:2–4, 11.

6   To investigate some of the evidence for this, see 'Resurrection—Fact or Fiction?', *BeThinking*. Available at: https://www.bethinking.org/booklets/resurrection-fact-or-fiction.

7   Revelation 21:1–4.

8   Matthew 6:19–21.

Chapter 22

1   Stephen Marche, 'Is Facebook Making Us Lonely?', *The Atlantic* (15 May 2012). Available at: http://www.theatlantic.com/magazine/archive/2012/05/is-facebook-making-us-lonely/308930/.

2   Cited in Paul Duncan (ed), *Stanley Kubrick: The Complete Films* (Taschen, 2011), p. 9.

3   Cited in Walter Hooper, *C.S. Lewis: The Companion and Guide* (Harper-Collins, 2005), p. 177.

Chapter 23

1   Thomas Nagel, *What Does It All Mean?: A Very Short Introduction to Philosophy* (Oxford University Press, 1987), p. 96.

2   John 1:1–3.

3   John 1:14.

Chapter 24

1   You can also watch a compelling dramatisation of the conversation between Jesus and Nicodemus in the seventh episode of the first season of *The Chosen*; see: https://www.youtube.com/watch?v=Q1AyMD-ZNy9k.

2   John 3:3.

3   John 3:4–5.

4   Mike Cain, *Real Life Jesus* (IVP, 2008), p. 63.

5   John 3:16–17.

Chapter 25

1   Bart D. Ehrman, *Did Jesus Exist? The Historical Argument for Jesus of Nazareth* (HarperCollins, 2012), p. 5.

2   John Dickson, *Is Jesus History?* (The Good Book Company, 2021).

3   Lucian, *The Works of Lucian of Samosata* , Vol. 4, chapters xi-xiii (1949), quoted in Gary Habermas, *The Historical Jesus* (College Press, 2008), p. 206.

4   Celsus, *On the True Doctrine: A Discourse Against the Christians*, trans. R. Joseph Hoffmann (Oxford University Press, 1987), p. 116. Quoted in: Ed J. Komoszeki, James M. Sawyer, and Daniel B. Wallace, *Reinventing Jesus* (Kregel Publications, 2006), p. 197.

5   Peter Kreeft 'Why I Believe Jesus Is The Son Of God' in Norman L. Geisler and Paul K. Hoffman (eds), *Why I Am a Christian: Leading Thinkers Explain Why They Believe* (Baker Books, 2001), pp. 240–241.

6   Mark 1:1.

7   Mark 8:29.

8   Mark 15:39.

9   Mark 16:8.

Chapter 26

1   'The Changing Global Religious Landscape', *Pew Research Center* (5 April 2017).

2   Quoted in Peter A. Georgescu, 'Exchange Religion for Faith', *Huffington Post* (14 Nov 2013). Available at: www.huffingtonpost.com/peter-a-georgesco/religion-and-faith_b_4265454.html.

3   I cover these differences in much greater detail in Andy Bannister, *Do Muslims and Christians Worship the Same God?* (IVP, 2021).

4   Matthew 7:7.

Chapter 27

1   See the 'Talking Jesus 2022 Research Report'. Available at: https://talkingjesus.org/2022-research/.

2   Josh Howarth, 'Alarming Average Screen Time Statistic (2023)', *Exploding Topics* (13 January 2023). Available at: https://explodingtopics.com/blog/screen-time-stats.

3   Ravi Shankar, 'Principles of Karma and Suffering', *Wisdom by Sri Sri Ravi Shankar*. Available at: https://wisdom.srisriravishankar.org/principles-of-karma-and-suffering/.

4   Acts 16:27.

Chapter 28

1   Aleksandr Solzhenitsyn, *The Gulag Archipelago,* Vol. 1 (Collins/Harvill, 1982 [1973]), p. 168.

2   Joseph Burgo, 'Why Most People Don't Really Change', *After Psychology* (4 October 2010). Available at https://www.afterpsychotherapy.com/no-change/.

3   John 8:12.

4   Read his story in Thomas A. Tarrants, *Consumed by Hate, Redeemed by Love: How a Violent Klansman Became a Champion of Racial Reconciliation* (Nelson Books, 2019).

5   Matthew Parris, 'As an Atheist, I Truly Believe Africa Needs God', *The Times* (27 December 2008). Available at: https://www.thetimes.co.uk/article/as-an-atheist-i-truly-believe-africa-needs-god-3xj9b-m80h8m.

Conclusion

1   The original version of the scene can be found in J.R.R. Tolkien, *The Fellowship of the Ring*, 'A Journey in the Dark', book 2, chapter 4.

2   Douglas Coupland, *Life After God* (Pocket Books, 1995), p. 359.

Contributors

Andy Bannister

Dr Andy Bannister is a speaker, writer, broadcaster, and director of Solas. He has written several books, including *The Atheist Who Didn't Exist (or The Terrible Consequences of Bad Arguments)* and *Do Muslims and Christians Worship the Same God?*. Andy holds a PhD in Islamic Studies and enjoys engaging with people of all faiths and none about life's big questions. He lives in Wiltshire with his wife Astrid and their two young children. Andy enjoys hillwalking, travel, and telling dad jokes.

Gareth Black

Gareth Black is a civil servant, speaker, and writer. He holds degrees in Theology from the University of Oxford and in Bioethics from King's College London. He is also an associate tutor in Ethics at the University of Cumbria. Gareth lives in Belfast with his wife and son, and in his spare time enjoys playing sport, music, and reading.

Gavin Matthews

Gavin Matthews is a writer, speaker, editor, and an assistant director of Solas. He has degrees in Theology, Political Science and History, and a Master's degree in Modern American History and Politics from St Andrews. Gavin lives in Perth, Scotland with his wife Elaine. They have three adult children. When not working he enjoys hillwalking, reading, photography, and music.

Andy Moore

Andy Moore currently serves as the vice principal of Finance and Portfolio Performance for Talanton, an impact investment fund. Andy is an adjunct speaker at OCCA and has spoken about faith at some of the world's largest companies, including Facebook, UBS, KPMG, and Barclays. Andy holds a degree in Corporate Management from Northumbria University and a Master's in Philosophy from the University of Birmingham. Andy is married to Rachel and lives near Oxford.

David Nixon

David Nixon is a pastor at Carrubbers Christian Centre on Edinburgh's Royal Mile. After studying Law at the University of Edinburgh, David went on to study Theology at the Faith Mission Bible College and London School of Theology. David is a husband to Kirsty and father to two energetic young boys.

Michael Ots

Michael Ots is a speaker and author. He travels widely around the UK, Europe, and Eurasia speaking mainly on university campuses around issues of life and faith. He is the author of four books, the first of which, *What kind of God?*, was nominated for a major UK book award and has been translated into seven languages. Michael studied in Scotland, lives in Leicestershire, England, and is married to Rebecca, an airline pilot.

Mary Jo Sharp

A former atheist who came to faith, Mary Jo Sharp is now an assistant professor of Apologetics at Houston Christian University, and the founder and director of Confident Christianity Apologetics Ministry. She is the author of several books, including *Why I Still Believe: A Former Atheist's Reckoning with the Bad Reputation Christians Give a Good God*. Mary Jo lives with her husband and family in Portland, Oregon.

Andy Steiger

Dr Andy Steiger is the founder of Apologetics Canada. He is the author of *Reclaimed: How Jesus Restores Our Humanity in a Dehumanized World*. Recently, Andy completed a new video series, called *Branded: A Series on Identity*, that addresses our personal, communal, and spiritual identity. Andy holds a PhD from the University of Aberdeen in Scotland and currently lives in British Columbia, Canada, with his wife Nancy and their two boys.

Clare Williams

Clare Williams is the founder of Real Questions, an organisation that looks at faith and the black British experience. She studied English Language and Literature at the University of Oxford before working in education for ten years. Clare also holds an MA in Culture, Diaspora, and Ethnicity from Birkbeck, University of London. Clare lives in London where she is currently researching a PhD in Sociology at Westminster University.

Anne Witton

Anne Witton is a writer and speaker based in Newcastle who has spent many years in full-time mission work. She studied Philosophy at University College London, has a Master's in Contemporary Missiology and is the former Content Director at Living Out. Anne loves wild swimming, samba drumming, books, and playing her ukulele.

Acknowledgements

Andy Bannister and Gavin Matthews would like to thank all the contributors to *Have You Ever Wondered?* who have invested huge amounts of time, energy, creativity and commitment in this project. We would also like to thank the wonderful editorial team at 10Publishing, who have been a joy to work with and who didn't manage to remove all of Andy's jokes from the final script! We both owe a significant debt of gratitude to our amazing colleagues at Solas for their friendship and partnership in all that we do, with a special mention for the late Jeff Howarth to whom this volume is dedicated. Finally, we would like to thank our respective families for their ongoing encouragement and heckling from offstage.

More books from 10Publishing

Resources that point to Jesus

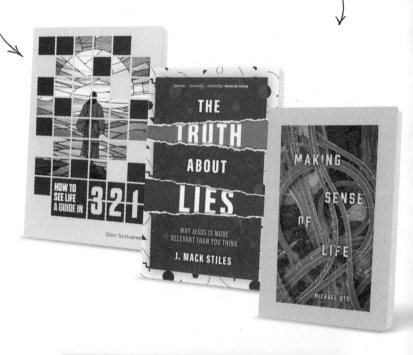